Grace
for
Grief

Grace for Grief

Daily Comfort for Those Who Mourn

WORLD PUBLISHING

Grand Rapids, Michigan 49418 U.S.A.

Scripture text for *Grace for Grief* is taken from GOD'S WORD.
GOD'S WORD is a trademark of God's Word to the Nations Bible
Society and is used by permission. GOD'S WORD is the name for **The
Holy Bible: God's Word to the Nations**, copyright © 1994 by
God's Word to the Nations Bible Society. All rights reserved.

Published by World Bible Publishers, Inc., Grand Rapids, MI 49418

Book design by Scott Pinzon & Richard Brimer, Pinpoint Marketing, WA

ISBN 0-529-10479-2 (paperback)
ISBN 0-529-10484-9 (hardcover)

Library of Congress Catalog Card Number: 95-61694

Printed in the United States of America

1 2 3 4 5 6 – 99 98 97 96 95

Dedication

To Mark
(February 1973 - April 1992)

and

to Jennifer Lynn
(May 1978 - December 1979)

You lit up our life, sweet children. You taught us about love and life, that pain and joy are not far separated, and that with much wisdom is much sorrow. We smile through our tears and grow through our pain, taking solace in the knowledge of our coming reunion in a joyous heaven. We love you!

Introduction

AS SURELY AS DAY follows night and spring follows winter, life does follow grief. If this is your first season of deep grief, you may be wondering if it will ever end and if life will return to normal. Well, the pain does pass, but the memories don't, and a life stretched by the pain of loss never returns to its original shape. In time, however, the memories that now rush tears to your eyes will one day, with those same tears, bring healing and a somewhat involuntary smile to your anguished heart.

Grief is a process, not an event. You can't avoid it. You can't rush it. It's a walk, one step at a time, and it takes time for this necessary process to bring healing and wholeness back to your life. After many painful experiences that brought grief to us, such as divorce, business failure and the death of our children, we came to depend on the comfort of God and his word to bring us through the fire.

Use this book as part of your daily quiet time. Let God's word speak to you and minister to you as you experience his grace through your journey. Grief is a normal part of life. It happens to everyone at one time or another. Don't rush it. Remember, there is hope. There is *Grace for Grief*.

Our heartfelt love and empathy,
Michael & Brenda Pink

8

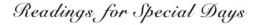

Readings for Special Days

Week 1

SUNDAY

"Even though I walk through the dark valley of death, because you are with me, I fear no harm. Your rod and your staff give me courage." (Psalm 23:4)

Lord, my senses are numb. I keep thinking that I will wake up and this will all be just a terrible dream. But I am awake, and this one that I love so much is gone, no longer here to cheer me with a smile or refresh me with an encouraging look. It feels like I'm walking through a dense fog in slow motion. Could this be the valley of the shadow of death?

Today's reading: 1 Corinthians 15

MONDAY

"This is too much work for you. You can't do it alone!" (Exodus 18:18)

I'm hearing from others who extend their sympathy and love, but when night comes, I am overwhelmed and feel incredibly alone. I just can't do it alone, Lord. I can't make it through the next few days without you. I need you to carry me through these extremely difficult days. Please help me.

Today's reading: Psalm 92

TUESDAY

"Trust the LORD with all your heart, and do not rely on your own understanding. In all your ways acknowledge him, and he will make your paths smooth." (Proverbs 3:5,6)

Lord, what has happened to my life? What will happen now? There is so much I don't understand, and some questions I am afraid to even ask. I know only one thing I can do: put my trust in you, for you are righteous and you alone know our hearts.

Today's reading: Psalm 40

WEDNESDAY

"But God told me, 'My kindness is all you need. My power is strongest when you are weak.' So I will brag even more about my weaknesses in order that Christ's power will live in me. Therefore, I accept weakness, mistreatment, hardship, persecution and difficulties suffered for Christ. It's clear that when I'm weak, I'm strong." (2 Corinthians 12:9,10)

At my weakest moment, I truly sensed your presence stronger and closer than at any time in my life. It was as if I had been anesthetized, yet fully conscious, and for a few strange moments I was comforting others. I don't understand how you did that, but at the most difficult times, I, though in pain, was numbed to that pain and passed through the day knowing I was aided by your grace, but not at all understanding it. Truly, in weakness, I became strong.

Today's reading: 2 Corinthians 1 & 2

THURSDAY

"Jesus said to her, 'I am the one who brings people back to life, and I am life itself. Those who believe in me will live even if they die. Everyone who lives and believes in me will never die. Do you believe that?'" (John 11:25)

Lord, I do believe that! I cling to that hope with all that is within me. It is that promise that gets me through the day and gives me hope for the future. Thank you for reassuring me that death for your children is merely a passage into a perfect world, where you will one day wipe away all our tears. Thank you for the Resurrection.

Today's reading: Romans 8

FRIDAY

"This is eternal life: to know you, the only true God, and Jesus Christ, whom you sent. God loved the world this way: He gave his only Son so that everyone who believes in him will not die but will have eternal life." (John 17:3, 3:16)

Father, thank you for loving me so much that you would let your son die for me. Knowing you means everything to me and gives me the assurance of seeing my loved one again and being together forever. Help me to remember this at all times.

Today's reading: John 3

SATURDAY

"My son, pay attention to my words. Open your ears to what I say. Do not lose sight of these things. Keep them deep within your heart because they are life to those who find them and they heal the whole body." (Proverbs 4:20–22)

Where else could I go for strength if I didn't have your words to comfort me? Your words nourish me and give me life. I will hold them deep within my heart and cherish them every moment of the day.

Today's reading: John 6

Week 2

S U N D A Y

"The Messenger of the LORD camps around those who fear him, and he rescues them. Their victory comes from the LORD. He is their fortress in times of trouble." (Psalm 34:7, 37:39)

Lord, amidst the noise of my troubled soul it seems that if I listen carefully, I can almost hear the rush of angel wings bringing a message of hope and victory. During those times of quiet anguish, I find security and comfort in your presence.

Today's reading: Hebrews 4

M O N D A Y

"The LORD is my light, my confidence, my rock, my savior, my strength, and my shield. My heart trusted him, so I received help. My heart is triumphant. I cannot be severely shaken, and I fear no harm." (Psalm 27:1, Proverbs 3:26, Psalm 62:2,, 28:7 23:4)

Lord, there are so many decisions that I feel unprepared to make. I need you to protect me from people or situations that could harm me. I turn to you today for every decision and need I have. Please light my path, shield my vulnerable soul and give me confidence to face the day.

Today's reading: Psalm 119

TUESDAY

"God faithfully keeps his promises. He called us to be partners with his Son Jesus Christ our Lord, and our relationship is with the Father and with his Son Jesus Christ, who is not ashamed to call us his brothers and sisters." (1 Corinthians 1:9, 1 John 1:3, Hebrews 2:11)

It's hard for me to imagine that you have called me to be a partner with your son Jesus, but you are faithful and always keep your promises. Jesus, I've just lost one of your partners here on earth and there is no one that could ever replace that special person. Please pour your Spirit into the void of my heart and remind me again that I am yours.

Today's reading: Psalm 103

WEDNESDAY

"Remain in God's love as you look for the mercy of our Lord Jesus Christ to give you eternal life, knowing that all things work together for the good of those who love God—those whom he has called according to his plan." (Jude 1:21, Romans 8:28)

Lord, today I ask you to send a friend to me to show me your tender love. I know you often show your love through your people and I need that kind of love today.

Today's reading: 1 John 5

Week 2

THURSDAY

"Now I know that the LORD will give victory to his anointed king. He will answer him from his holy heaven with mighty deeds of his powerful hand. Some rely on chariots and others on horses, but we will boast in the name of the LORD our God." (Psalm 20:6,7)

Father, I know that your promises to the saints of biblical times do not exceed the promises you make to us today. With this in mind, I ask only for a small victory, one that will get me through another day and on the path to recovery. I rely only on you, my Lord, and as you show yourself strong on my behalf, I know I will boast again in your mighty name.

Today's reading: Hebrews 6

FRIDAY

"The way of the LORD is a fortress for an innocent person. When you call on him, he answers you and makes you bold by strengthening your soul." (Proverbs 10:29, Psalm 138:3)

Lord, your steadfast love is my strength to face each new day while my wounded heart struggles to find the rhythm of life again. Though I can't really see the progress, I find myself having the courage to entertain fond memories before they

are washed away with my tears. This day is especially painful, for its happy memory is shrouded in a painful reality.
Strengthen my soul today!

Today's reading: Psalm 138

SATURDAY

*"May God, the source of hope, fill you with joy and peace through
your faith in him. Then you will overflow with hope by the power
of the Holy Spirit." (Romans 15:13)*

Lord, I am so thankful that you have given me hope so that I
do not grieve as those who have no hope. Hope is all I have.
Joy, for now, is but a fleeting memory and peace seems to
come and go, but I know that you are the source and I ask
you now with great hope in my heart, for both joy and peace.

Today's reading: Romans 5

Week 3

SUNDAY

"When you call to me, I will answer you. I will be with you when you are in trouble. I will save you and honor you. How precious are my thoughts concerning you!" (Psalm 91:15, 139:17)

Where have all my comforters gone? I have not recovered from this loss. They have gone back to life as usual, but my life will never be "as usual." It gives me great comfort to know that you, the God of the universe, think about me, answer me when I call, and are with me in troubled times. Thank you Lord for your gift of friendship.

Today's reading: Isaiah 51

MONDAY

"God arms me with strength and makes my way perfect. He makes my feet like those of a deer and gives me sure footing on high places." (Psalm 18:32,33)

Though I am having a hard time finding my way, you, Lord, make it right and set me on a steady path leading to wholeness. I'm told recovery is a long process, and I am trusting you to lead me through it at a pace I can handle.

Today's reading: Philippians 4

TUESDAY

"It is good to give thanks to the LORD, to make music to praise your name, O Most High. It is good to announce your mercy in the morning and your faithfulness in the evening..." (Psalm 92:,2)

Lord, it feels good to sit here and think of all the reasons I have to be thankful. Praise begins to well up in my heart as I think upon your mercy and meditate upon your great faithfulness. Lord, it's not always easy, but regardless of my feelings I will praise you and remember that you inhabit the praises of your people and that your presence brings joy.

Today's reading: Psalm 147

WEDNESDAY

"Yet, the strength of those who wait with hope in the Lord will be renewed. They will soar on wings like eagles. They will run and won't become weary. They will walk and won't grow tired." (Isaiah 40:31)

Some days it is so hard to keep going, and I know I can't do it in my own strength. So I wait, and in waiting I find you. And when I find, I find strength. When I find strength, I find courage and am ready to spread my wings and head back out into the storm again. Because of your wonderful promise to me of renewed strength, I will rise above the storm.

Today's reading: Isaiah 40

Week 3

THURSDAY

"Call to me, and I will answer you. I will tell you great and myste-rious things that you do not know." (Jeremiah 33:3)

Father, please tell me about heaven. Now that someone I love and miss so much is there, I want to know about heaven. I wish I could see the gates of that great city and walk the streets of gold, but more than all of that, I wish I could get a glimpse of my dear loved one just one more time. Maybe tonight Lord, in my dreams....

Today's reading: Revelation 21

FRIDAY

"But as Scripture says: No eye has seen, no ear has heard, and no mind has imagined the things that God has prepared for those who love him." (1 Corinthians 2:9)

I'm still thinking about heaven; and to think that nobody has ever seen, heard or imagined the things you have prepared for us! What kind of wonderful place can it be? I long for the day when I will both see and hear the things you have pre-pared for me. Thank you for loving me that much.

Today's reading: Revelation 22

SATURDAY

"Be wise in the way you act toward those who are outside the Christian faith. Make the most of your opportunities. Everything you say should be kind and well thought out so that you know how to answer everyone." (Colossians 4: 5,6)

Lord, though I sorrow deeply, I have so much hope that only you can give. I know others have observed the peace that has come to me in waves and wonder at its source. Please give me opportunity to share with them your love, that they may find your peace too.

Today's reading: Colossians 1

Week 4

SUNDAY

"With perfect peace you will protect those whose minds cannot be changed, because they trust you, and we have peace with God because of what our Lord Jesus Christ has done." (Isaiah 26:3, Romans 5:1)

Father, as I review the current circumstances, I keep coming back to one reassuring fact: this one that I love so much is safe with you. I find peace in the certainty of what Jesus did for us all, and one day I know we will be together again. Though I am at great peace with this fact, it does not preclude me from feeling the pain of separation now. Thank you for helping me through the pain.

Today's reading: 1 Peter 1

MONDAY

"Ask the LORD for rain in the springtime. The LORD makes thunderstorms. He gives everyone rain showers for the plants in the field." (Zechariah 10:1)

Lord, I am in a dry and thirsty place in my life, too weak to refresh myself. Please rain your refreshing presence on my life. Let me sense your nearness and experience your great kindness again today. Let it rain, let it pour! Let me hear your positive affirmation in the empty recesses of my heart.

Today's reading: Joel 2:18–32

TUESDAY

"As long as the earth exists, planting and harvesting, cold and heat, summer and winter, day and night will never stop. Weeping may last for the night, but there is a song of joy in the morning."
(Genesis 8:22, Psalm 30:5)

Father, as surely as springtime follows winter, and day follows night, joy will follow sorrow. I feel like I'm in a season of night during the dead of winter, yet I know this season will pass and songs of joy will once again flow from my lips. But right now, Lord, it's dark and cold and lonely. Please put a song in my heart to remind me that springtime is coming, that the light of day is near and joy will one day return like the spring flowers.

Today's reading: Ecclesiastes 3:1–8

Week 4

WEDNESDAY

"Hear, O LORD, and have pity on me! O LORD, be my helper! You have changed my sobbing into dancing. You have removed my sackcloth and clothed me with joy so that my soul may praise you with music and not be silent." (Psalm 30:10,11)

Though I have yet to experience this change I thank you, Father, that I have it to look forward to. One day, I will be so overcome with joy that I will not be able to keep silent and will praise you with all my heart. Start the changing process now, Lord. Give me a glimpse of what is to be, that I may begin praising you more each day.

Today's reading: Psalm 16

THURSDAY

"Make your water spring up! Sing to the well, the well dug by princes, dug out by the nobles of the people with their scepters and staffs." (Numbers 21:17,18)

You have placed a well of water in my soul, but right now, Lord, it feels like it has dried up. I would like to sing, but I have no song today. I would like to be refreshed, but I can't get water from my well. But I will sing anyway, and as I sing, please cause the water to spring up and refresh my spirit and renew my soul.

Today's reading: 1 Chronicles 16

FRIDAY

"Today I'm giving you the choice of a blessing or a curse. You'll be blessed if you obey the commands of the LORD your God that I'm giving you today. You'll be cursed if you disobey the commands of the LORD your God, if you turn from the way I'm commanding you to live today, and if you worship other gods you never knew." (Deuteronomy 11:26–28)

Who else could ever merit the worship that you alone deserve? I purpose with conviction to learn your commands, your way of life, and to follow you. I choose your blessing.

Today's reading: Exodus 20

SATURDAY

"Naked I came from my mother, and naked I will return. The LORD has given, and the LORD has taken away! May the name of the LORD be praised." (Job 1:21)

Lord, it has been nearly a month since I suffered this loss. I still haven't come to understand it, but I do know that I, too, will one day follow in that path. All life comes from you and you appoint our days. Today, in the midst of my unanswered questions, I praise you!

Today's reading: Psalm 34

Week 5

SUNDAY

"Brace yourself like a man! I will ask you, and you will teach me. Would you undo my justice? Would you condemn me so that you can be righteous?" (Job 40:7,8)

Lord, forgive me for accusing you or challenging your justice. I know you are righteous and yet I still grapple to understand the unwanted changes in my life. Nevertheless, I choose today to trust you with my unanswered questions.

Today's reading: 2 Samuel 22

MONDAY

"Blessed is the person who does not follow the advice of wicked people, take the path of sinners, or join the company of mockers. Rather, he delights in the teachings of the LORD and reflects on his teachings day and night." (Psalm 1:1,2)

Lord, I have received so much advice from so many people, but what I am looking for is wisdom. Teach me, out of your word, principles which I can use to govern the many decisions I must make. Bring godly counsel across my path to assist in this process.

Today's reading: Psalm 18

TUESDAY

"O LORD, look how my enemies have increased! Many are attacking me. Many are saying about me, 'Even with God on his side, he won't be victorious.'" (Psalm 3:1,2)

Lord, though the voices of despair taunt me in my weak moments, I know that with you on my side I can do all things because Jesus Christ strengthens me. I will experience your victory despite the forces that seem to have rallied against me.

Today's reading: Psalm 31

WEDNESDAY

"Even if the fig tree does not bloom and the vines have no grapes, even if the olive tree fails to produce and the fields yield no food, even if the sheep pen is empty and the stalls have no cattle—even then, I will be happy with the LORD. I will truly find joy in God, who saves me." (Habakkuk 3:17,18)

Father, I find in loss the one thing I can never lose, and that is your love for me. No matter what my lot in life, I can truly sing, it is well with my soul Even when sorrow, like sea billows, flows over me, I find happiness in you who saves me. Though there is so much I don't understand, I am finding it less and less important to have answers and more and more important to have you.

Today's reading: Song of Songs 2

THURSDAY

"No weapon that has been made to be used against you will succeed. You will have an answer for anyone who accuses you. This is the inheritance of the LORD's servants. Their victory comes from me, declares the LORD." (Isaiah 54:17)

It seems that this loss is being wielded against me like a weapon and is striking at the very cord of my existence, but it will not succeed. Rather, Lord, use this painful experience to reveal more of you to me: more of your nature, your goodness and your faithfulness. Give me an answer for destructive thoughts that at times assail my soul. As your servant, I thank you for this promised inheritance.

Today's reading: Psalm 91

FRIDAY

"Preserve justice, and do what is right. My salvation is about to come. My righteousness is about to be revealed." (Isaiah 56:1)

Bring your salvation, Lord. I know you will do what is right and just. Reveal your righteousness to me and cause me to be a good reflection of you to others, especially those affected by this loss. These new circumstances bring with them new trials and even temptations. Please help me to do what is right.

Today's reading: James 1

SATURDAY

"Rain and snow come down from the sky. They do not go back again Oproduces seed for farmers and food for people to eat. My word, which comes from my mouth, is like the rain and snow. It will not come back to me without results, but it will accomplish whatever I want and achieve whatever I send it to do." (Isaiah 55:10,11)

Send your word like the rain to my soul. Make it cool as the snow. Refresh my innermost being and make me like a well-watered garden, bringing forth fruit in the coming days. Lord, please send your word into my heart and allow it to produce the things you desire.

Today's reading: Isaiah 55

Week 6

SUNDAY

"You will go out with joy and be led out in peace. The mountains and the hills will break into songs of joy in your presence, and all the trees will clap their hands. Cypress trees will grow where thorn bushes grew. Myrtle trees will grow where briars grew. This will be a reminder of the Lord's name and an everlasting sign that will never be destroyed." (Isaiah 55:12,13)

Father, I see so many thorn bushes in my life where once grew the mighty cypress. I take your promise that once again, strong, vibrant life will replace the petty, small briars so evident in my existence. I am finding it hard to imagine that my life will ever be even a shadow of what it once was, but I hold to your promise of new life.

Today's reading: Psalm 75

MONDAY

"I call your name from the deepest pit, O Lord. Listen to my cry for help. Don't close your ears when I cry out for relief. Be close at hand when I call to you. You told me not to be afraid. Plead my case for me, O Lord. Reclaim my life." (Lamentations 3:55–58)

Today I came across a familiar piece of clothing tucked away in a place I'd thought I would never look. Streams of tears rushed down my face in almost uncontrollable sobs. I thought I was getting somewhat better then suddenly, without warning, a powerful reminder of an irreplaceable past paraded in front of me. And I am reminded once again of a loss I can only accept, and never replace.

Today's reading: Isaiah 40

TUESDAY

"What do you think? Suppose a man has 100 sheep and one of them strays. Won't he leave the 99 sheep in the hills to look for the one that has strayed? I can guarantee this: if he finds it, he is happier about it than about the 99 that have not strayed. In the same way, your Father in heaven does not want one of these little ones to be lost." (Matthew 18:12–14)

Today I feel like that one sheep that has strayed from the ninety-nine. The wolves are howling, the wind is cruel and the food is scarce. You are my Shepherd and I know you will leave the ninety-nine to come and rescue me. In that knowledge, I will rest.

Today's reading: Psalm 35

WEDNESDAY

"I can guarantee again that if two of you agree on anything here on earth, my Father in heaven will accept it. Where two or three have come together in my name, I am there among them." (Matthew 18:19,20)

Father, please bring someone by that can agree with your word and pray with me that your will be done, in my life, just as your will is accomplished in heaven. We shall join together in your name and welcome your presence as we seek your will.

Today's reading: Matthew 6

THURSDAY

"After they had hit Paul and Silas many times, they threw them in jail and ordered the jailer to keep them under tight security. So the jailer followed these orders and put Paul and Silas into solitary confinement with their feet in leg irons. Around midnight Paul and Silas were praying and singing hymns of praise to God." (Acts 16:23–25)

Just when I think I've got it bad, I read how the fathers of our faith lived and died. In the midst of their ordeals they found praise in their heart for you, Lord. Today, I will praise your name and sing to you, making melody in my heart for all the great things you have done.

Today's reading: Psalm 75

FRIDAY

"Brothers and sisters, because of God's compassion toward us, I encourage you to offer your bodies as living sacrifices, dedicated to God and pleasing to him. This kind of worship is appropriate for you." (Romans 12:1)

Father, it is both an honor and a privilege to offer my whole being to you as a living sacrifice. I don't know what my future holds or even what path I should take, but I offer my life to you in worshipful appreciation for all you have done for me.

Today's reading: Psalm 42

SATURDAY

"Don't become like the people of this world. Instead, change the way you think. Then you will always be able to determine what God really wants—what is good, pleasing and perfect." (Romans 12:2)

Lord, as I spend time in your word, cause me to perceive the world I live in through your paradigm. Open up my understanding as I read today and help me change the way I think, so that I can recognize your will and walk perfectly in your ways.

Today's reading: Romans 12

SUNDAY

"Though outwardly we are wearing out, inwardly we are renewed day by day. Our suffering is light and temporary and is producing for us an eternal glory that is greater than anything we can imagine." (2 Corinthians 4:16,17)

Thank you, Lord, for the work of renewal I can sense happening in my heart. My suffering has seemed anything but light or temporary, yet as surely as this will one day pass, it will also seem one day to have been light in comparison with the great glory you have in store.

Today's reading: Proverbs 2

MONDAY

"We don't look for things that can be seen but for things that can't be seen. Things that can be seen are only temporary. But things that can't be seen last forever." (2 Corinthians 4:18)

Before my loss, I could see, feel, and hear the one I loved, but that was all so temporary. Now that I can no longer see this one, I know that the one I loved will last forever. When I too pass into God's presence, I will see then what I cannot see now. I anxiously await that day!

Today's reading: Psalm 103

TUESDAY

"You received a gift from God when I placed my hands on you to ordain you. Now I'm reminding you to fan that gift into flames. God didn't give us a cowardly spirit but a spirit of power, love, and good judgment." (2 Timothy 1:6,7)

I wish you would fan my gifts into flames, but you have put that responsibility on me. Therefore, I will stir myself up, praying with the Holy Spirit's help, which gives me confidence and power to do the things you have called me to do. Today, by your grace, I will walk in love and sound judgment.

Today's reading: Psalm 104

WEDNESDAY

"This is a statement that can be trusted: If we have died with him, we will live with him. If we endure, we will rule with him. If we disown him, he will disown us. If we are unfaithful, he remains faithful because he cannot be untrue to himself." (2 Timothy 2:11–13)

The knowledge that the one I have lost now lives with you enables me to endure this present hardship. To know that I will one day rule with you is somehow beyond my scope as I struggle here just to rule my own emotions. Thank you for being faithful to me, even when I have been unfaithful to you.

Today's reading: Deuteronomy 7

THURSDAY

"So if you call God your Father, live your time as temporary residents on earth in fear." (1 Peter 1:17)

When I was young, I thought I was indestructible and wanted to live forever. Now I am older, at times nearly destroyed, and the temporary nature of life is now a welcome thought. Not that I want to depart early, but I eagerly look for a home with foundations whose builder and maker is God.

Today's reading: 1 Corinthians 2

FRIDAY

"God's word is active. It is sharper than any two-edged sword and cuts as deep as the place where soul and spirit meet, the place where joints and marrow meet. God's word judges a person's thoughts and intentions." (Hebrews 4:12)

Judge my heart, O Lord, and purify my intentions. Look deep within the secret places of my heart and see if there be any sin in me. I want to serve you in such a way as to enhance your reputation here on earth. Teach me how to dispense your word with power and love to others who are in need.

Today's reading: Psalm 139

SATURDAY

"Then the Lord said, 'Simon, Simon, listen! Satan has demanded to have you apostles for himself. He wants to separate you from me as a farmer separates wheat from husks. But I have prayed for you, Simon, that your faith will not fail. So when you recover, strengthen the other disciples.' " (Luke 22:31,32)

Father, at times I feel separated from you and at the mercy of an unmerciful enemy. But I know that you are constantly praying for me, and my faith will not fail. Lord, when I recover from this loss, I will strengthen others who are going through the process of grief. I will encourage them as you have encouraged me.

Today's reading: 2 Corinthians 1

SUNDAY

"The days are going to come, declares the Lord, when the one who plows will catch up to the one who harvests, and the one who stomps on grapes will catch up to the one who plants. New wine will drip from the mountains and flow from all the hills. I will restore my people Israel." (Amos 9:13,14)

Father, your word is so rich with promise I can turn almost anywhere and find courage to face another day. My life was so suddenly disrupted and permanently changed that I thought my wounds would never heal. Today, I looked at some old photos and smiled through glassy eyes as I realized I am beginning to heal.

Today's reading: Amos 9

MONDAY

"Break out into shouts of joy, ruins of Jerusalem. The Lord will comfort his people. He will reclaim Jerusalem. The Lord will show his holy power to all the nations." (Isaiah 52:9)

I feel like the ruins of Jerusalem. Today, I will encourage myself in the Lord until joy breaks through in my spirit. I will shout for joy, for you are reclaiming me and rebuilding my life. You will show your power on my behalf.

Today's reading: Philippians 4:8

TUESDAY

"You will search for your enemies, but you will not find them. Those who are at war with you will be reduced to nothing and no longer exist. I, the Lord your God, hold your right hand and say to you, 'Don't be afraid; I will help you.'" (Isaiah 41:12,13)

Today I receive your help with outstretched hand. I will not be afraid, though I've never been down this path before. The forces that rage against me are losing their power as my faith in you grows and your love in me increases.

Today's reading: Isaiah 40

WEDNESDAY

"Righteous people flourish like palm trees and grow tall like the cedars in Lebanon. They are planted in the Lord's house. They blossom in our God's courtyards. Even when they are old, they still bear fruit." (Psalm 92:12–14)

Father, you have made me righteous through your son Jesus Christ and now, though I would like to flourish, I would be happy today for marginal improvement. Please don't give up on me but cause me to blossom, to bear fruit and to become viable again in my own sight.

Today's reading: James 5:7–20

THURSDAY

"This is the word the Lord spoke to Zerubbabel: 'You won't succeed by might or by power, but by my Spirit, says the Lord of Armies.'" (Zechariah 4:6)

Today I cease trying to hasten the recovery process by pretending that I'm fine now. I'm only suppressing what will one day burst forth. Teach me by your Spirit, Lord, how to walk under the reign of your Spirit through the pain.

Today's reading: 2 Corinthians 10

FRIDAY

"Let's return to the Lord. Even though he has torn us to pieces, he will heal us. Even though he has wounded us, he will bandage our wounds." (Hosea 6:1)

The more I know you, Lord, the less I understand you and the more I marvel at your greatness. I stand in awe, dumbstruck by what I see in your word, but somehow I'm drawn closer to you and humbled by your presence. Please bandage my wounds and hasten the healing process.

Today's reading: 1 Thessalonians 3

SATURDAY

"Let's learn about the Lord. Let's get to know the Lord. He will come to us as sure as the morning comes. He will come to us like the autumn rains and the spring rains that water the ground."
(Hosea 6:3)

Father, I have so many preconceived ideas about you. During this storm in my life, many are being washed away. There seems to be little left standing but your grace, your mercy and your love. The rest that I thought I knew has been shaken. Please teach me about you and help me to learn. Come to me like a fresh rain and cause growth to begin again.

Today's reading: 2 Timothy 2

Week 9

SUNDAY

"Everything has its own time, and there is a specific time for every activity under heaven: a time to be born and a time to die, a time to plant and a time to pull out what was planted." (Ecclesiastes 3:1,2)

Father, help me settle this issue in my heart, that everyone has a time to be born and to die. Help me to accept what I cannot change. Show me when to put down roots and when it's time to move on. I wonder, should I make major changes or simply plant and drive my roots deeper? Until I know for sure, I believe I will bloom where you have me planted.

Today's reading: Proverbs 8

MONDAY

"... a time to kill and a time to heal, a time to tear down and a time to build up..." (Ecclesiastes 3:3)

I've already experienced the loss of someone dear; it must be time for healing to progress. What we had built in life has been torn down. Show me how to build my life again. It seems whenever I start to build, the work ceases due to a faulty foundation. Please establish me again as a whole person that I may be able to believe that rebuilding is even possible.

Today's reading: Luke 6

TUESDAY

"... a time to cry and a time to laugh, a time to mourn and a time to dance..." (Ecclesiastes 3:4)

I know there's a time to cry and to laugh, to mourn and to dance, but why does everybody seem to think that the time for crying and mourning should be over? I can't laugh and dance this soon after such a tremendous loss. Yes, I know my loved one is happy. It's me who suffers the loss. I want to be able to laugh and dance, but it's not within me. Lord, thank you for allowing me time to grieve.

Today's reading: John 11:1–44

WEDNESDAY

"... a time to scatter stones and a time to gather them, a time to hug and a time to stop hugging..." (Ecclesiastes 3:5)

A hug! What I'd give for a hug from my dear one who is now with you, Lord! There is no other hug on earth that can replace that hug. I wish I could get an unconditional fatherly "love hug" from you, Lord. I need your love, Father, expressed through a fellow Christian. Please hug me through someone today.

Today's reading: Proverbs 18:24

THURSDAY

"... a time to start looking and a time to stop looking, a time to keep and a time to throw away..." (Ecclesiastes 3:6)

Is it time to put away some things, Lord? I can't bear to put them all away, but perhaps it's time to put some away. What should I keep? What should I give away? What should I throw away? This is a very difficult thing to walk through, and I'm not sure I can do it. I want to be alone, yet I desperately need someone to be with me. Please help me through this process.

Today's reading: 1 Peter 5

FRIDAY

"... a time to tear apart and a time to sew together, a time to keep quiet and a time to speak out..." (Ecclesiastes 3:7)

The fabric of my life has been torn apart, Lord, and I would like to see it begin to be sewn back together again. The stitches will always be a constant reminder of what once was, but I will use them to remind me of Joseph's coat of many colors which was an outward manifestation of his father's great love. In remembering that, I take comfort in your love, Father.

Today's reading: Genesis 37

SATURDAY

"... a time to love and a time to hate, a time for war and a time for peace." (Ecclesiastes 3:8)

You have said that to fear the Lord is to hate evil, and that I do. You have also demonstrated your love for me by allowing Christ to die for me while I was still a sinner. Teach me, Lord, to love the evil doer while hating the evil being done. Help me to know my battle is not with people, but with unseen forces which can be subdued in your name. Help me bring them the peace you have so freely given me.

Today's reading: 2 Corinthians 10:3–5

Week 10

SUNDAY

"Remember these things, Jacob: you are my servant, Israel. I formed you; you are my servant. Israel, I will not forget you, for I have reclaimed you. I formed you in the womb." (Isaiah 44:21,24)

Father, it's been almost two months and everybody seems to think I should be "over it" by now. I'm only over the shock itself, not the loss. People who said they would keep in touch avoid me like a leper. When I do run into them, they act like nothing has changed, when in fact nothing for me is the same! Thank you for not forgetting me and for reclaiming me from hopelessness.

Today's reading: Isaiah 49:15–18, Psalm 139

MONDAY

"Cling to discipline. Do not relax your grip on it. Keep it because it is your life. Do not stray onto the path of wicked people. Avoid it." (Proverbs 4:13,14)

I'm finding that just getting into the pattern of basic routines is actually helping me. Getting up in the morning and going about my daily business, though somewhat of a drudgery, is actually a blessing. It keeps me from straying where I do not need to be, and it keeps my mind on other things, even if those things are somewhat trivial. The distraction is a relief. Thank you for the opportunity to occupy my mind with other things.

Today's reading: Philippians 4:6–9

TUESDAY

"The fear of the Lord is a fountain of life to turn one away from the grasp of death." (Proverbs 14:27)

I had no idea how death could reach beyond the grave to pull in its next victim. I had given in to its deadly pull when you unexpectedly brought me to your fountain of life. Thank you for teaching me to fear the Lord and freeing me from the untimely grasp of death.

Today's reading: Colossians 3

WEDNESDAY

"Generations come, and generations go, but the earth lasts forever. Whatever has happened before will happen again. Whatever has been done before will be done again. There is nothing new under the sun." (Ecclesiastes 1:4,9)

Grief is not new to mankind, even great grief, but it is new to me. Nothing could have prepared me for grief other than grief itself. I wish I could go through life without the benefit of this lesson, but I'm sure I would have less to offer this world. Though at the present I feel I have very little indeed to offer, one day perhaps I will help a fellow struggler along life's path.

Today's reading: Romans 8

THURSDAY

"I look up toward the mountains. Where can I find help? My help comes from the Lord, the maker of heaven and earth. He will not let you fall. Your guardian will not fall asleep. Indeed, the Guardian of Israel never rests or sleeps. The Lord is your guardian." (Psalm 121:1–5)

Father, thank you for encouraging me today with your word. I need to know that as I walk down the path of recovery, you will watch over me night and day to keep me from falling.

Today's reading: John 16

FRIDAY

"I am suffering and in pain. Let your saving power protect me, O God. I want to praise the name of God with a song. I want to praise its greatness with a song of thanksgiving. This will please

the Lord more than sacrificing an ox or a bull with horns and hoofs."
(Psalm 69:29–31)

Father, if King David could have such a strong desire to praise
you in the midst of his suffering and pain, then surely I can
find a way to offer you thanks. As I sit here and deliberately
think of things I can thank you for, my list gets longer and
longer and my heart gets lighter and lighter. Praise your holy
name forevermore.

Today's reading: Psalm 84

SATURDAY

"Stop storing up treasures for yourselves on earth, where moths and
rust destroy and thieves break in and steal. Instead, store up trea-
sures for yourselves in heaven, where moths and rust don't destroy
and thieves don't break in and steal. Your heart will be where your
treasure is." (Matthew 6:19–21)

Indeed, I do have such treasure in heaven—the one I love so
much is there! I have set my mind on things above and am less
concerned about things below. Thank you for the promise to see
my loved one again. My heart indeed is where my treasure is.

Today's reading: Proverbs 3

SUNDAY

"Ask, and you will receive. Search, and you will find. Knock, and the door will be opened for you. Everyone who asks will receive. The one who searches will find, and for the one who knocks, the door will be opened." (Matthew 7:7,8)

Today I come to you Father asking for grace to get me through the day. I always have difficulty with special days like this because they bring back so many memories. On a day I should be celebrating, I am bracing for an emotional parachute jump without the parachute. Everyone is so happy, and I'm expected to be happy too, but inside it's all I can do to politely smile.

Today's reading: Hebrews 4

MONDAY

"Love sincerely. Hate evil. Hold on to what is good." (Romans 12:9)

Father, sometimes in my efforts to survive I have found myself throwing out the good with the bad. Not wanting to feel the pain, I have avoided discussing the many good memories. Help me to embrace what is good and not dwell on that which is not. When I'm with other people, I know it is both healthy and helpful to recall fond memories and even to laugh. Help me to laugh again. Help me to love again.

Today's reading: Nehemiah 8

TUESDAY

"Don't be lazy in showing your devotion. Use your energy to serve the Lord." (Romans 12:11)

I am devoted to you, Lord. Please show me ways that I can use my extra time to be a positive influence on others around me. I don't feel overly energetic, yet I know that I always feel better after I have accomplished something worthwhile. Today, lead me to find an activity that will help someone else and glorify you.

Today's reading: Matthew 5

WEDNESDAY

"Be happy in your confidence, be patient in trouble, and pray continually." (Romans 12:12)

I want to be happy and I am trying to be patient. Perhaps if I spent more time in quiet with you I could draw from your streams of joy and endure troubled times with patience. Father, I pray right now for increased confidence to approach you for any matter, knowing that I can call on your name day or night, free from the condemnation the enemy of my soul so lavishes upon me. Increase my faith. Strengthen me with your joy.

Today's reading: Psalm 5

THURSDAY

"Be happy with those who are happy. Be sad with those who are sad. Live in harmony with each other. Don't be arrogant, but be friendly to humble people." (Romans 12:15,16)

I never knew how important it was to be sad with those who were sad. For years, I mistakenly tried to "cheer" people up when what they really needed at the time was someone to empathize with them and to partake of their pain. Now I wish others understood this so they would allow me to be sad when I'm sad and to be happy when I feel happy. I guess people are doing the best they know how to do. Please help me live and love in harmony.

Today's reading: 1 John 4

FRIDAY

"Don't let evil conquer you, but conquer evil with good." (Romans 12:21)

The things the enemy has meant for evil, you can use for good. Though disaster struck my life, you can show me how to turn it into something good. By your grace, I will turn this nightmare into something that will benefit others, even if it just means being a more caring person. Change me, Father, into your image.

Today's reading: 1 Peter 5

SATURDAY

"Love is patient. Love is kind. Love isn't jealous. It doesn't sing its own praises. It isn't arrogant. It isn't rude. It doesn't think about itself. It isn't irritable. It doesn't keep track of wrongs." (1 Corinthians 13:4,5)

Fill me with this kind of love, Lord. All too often, I find myself absorbed with thinking about me and my losses. I become irritable, unkind and rude. Transform me on the inside. Spread your love in my heart by the Holy Spirit and forgive my transgressions. Thank you for not keeping track of my mistakes.

Today's reading: 1 Corinthians 13

Week 12

SUNDAY

"I can do everything through Christ who strengthens me because the one who is in me is greater than the one who is in the world. Everyone who has been born from God has won the victory over the world. Our faith is what wins the victory over the world." (Philippians 4:13, 1 John 4:4, 5:4)

Though my soul is weary and my heart grows faint, I know from where I draw my strength. In Christ alone, I place my faith and gain victory for the road ahead.

Today's reading: 1 John 5

MONDAY

"The righteous person has many troubles, but the LORD rescues him from all of them. Don't laugh at me, my enemies. Although I've fallen, I will get up. Although I sit in the dark, the LORD is my light." (Psalm 34:19, Micah 7:8)

All my afflictions pale in comparison to this, yet I know that you, Lord, will deliver me from the pain and anguish of this irreplaceable loss. Though in this life I will always feel a twinge of pain whenever I remember the darkness of this loss, you will uphold me, light my way and give me grace for the journey.

Today's reading: Psalm 34

TUESDAY

"Thank God that he gives us the victory, and always leads us in victory because of Christ, who stripped the rulers and authorities of their power and made a public spectacle of them." (1 Corinthians 15:57, 2 Corinthians 2:14, Colossians 2:15)

I am so thankful that as I give you thanks, you work on my behalf and cause me to triumph in Christ. When I feel overwhelmed by the forces of darkness, I am strengthened by the knowledge that you have won the victory over my foes and have given it to me to enjoy.

Today's Reading: I Corinthians 15

WEDNESDAY

"So place yourself under God's authority. Resist the devil, and he will run away from you. Don't let evil conquer you, but conquer evil with good. Be firm in the faith and resist him, knowing that other believers throughout the world are going through the same kind of suffering. If you faint in a crisis, you are weak." (James 4:7, Romans 12:21, 1 Peter 5:9, Proverbs 24:10)

Today I feel outgunned, outnumbered and all alone. The darkness within eclipses the sunlight without. Then it comes ... I remember your word and submit my thoughts and feelings to you. I resist the tormentor of my soul by drawing close to you and take heart that this path I walk, all people must walk. I am strengthened by the knowledge that you are with me always.

Today's reading: James 4

THURSDAY

"The victory for righteous people comes from the LORD. He is their fortress in times of trouble. He brings people under our authority and puts nations under our feet. With you we can walk over our enemies. With your name we can trample those who attack us."
(Psalm 37:39, Psalm 47:3, 44:5)

Today I feel your strength. I want to overcome the enemies of my soul, but when I try, I find that I'm not ready yet. Nevertheless, I feel your strength building back within me and know that in due time, I will be to full strength. In the meantime, Lord, please fight for me.

Today's reading: Psalm 44

FRIDAY

"A person's steps are directed by the LORD, and the LORD delights in his way. When he falls, he will not be thrown down headfirst because the LORD holds on to his hand. A righteous person may fall seven times, but he gets up again. However, in a disaster

wicked people fall, and will quickly dry up like grass and wither away like green plants." (Psalm 37:23,24, Proverbs 24:16, Psalm 37:2)

Even though you order my steps, it is normal to fall. Yet when I fall, you are always there to pick me up. It seems I have fallen a lot recently, but thank you for treating each time as though it were the first.

Today's reading: Psalm 37

SATURDAY

"I am convinced that nothing can ever separate us from God's love which Christ Jesus our Lord shows us. We can't be separated by death or life, by angels or rulers, by anything in the present or anything in the future, by forces or powers in the world above or in the world below, or by anything else in creation." (Romans 8:38,39)

My friends ignore my pain in their futile effort to "not make me think about it," and the world around me seems particularly cold and unfeeling. Though my family does not wish to discuss our loss and those closest to me seem so far off, I am greatly comforted by the fact that nothing in heaven or earth will ever separate me from your blanket of love. Today, I wrap myself in that blanket.

Today's reading: Romans 8

SUNDAY

"Don't ever worry and say, 'What are we going to eat?' or 'What are we going to drink?' or 'What are we going to wear?' But first, be concerned about God's kingdom and what has his approval. Then all these things will be provided for you." (Matthew 6:31,33)

This loss causes me to rethink what I value most. Nothing is more important than seeking you and your kingdom. My life is but a vapor that appears for a little time. All that matters is what I do for your kingdom.

Today's reading: Matthew 6

MONDAY

"He pulled me out of a horrible pit, out of the mud and clay. He set my feet on a rock and made my steps secure." (Psalm 40:2)

Thank you, Father, for saving my soul and giving me eternal life. Death is only a passing into the spiritual realm, where life really is located.

Today's reading: Psalm 42

TUESDAY

"Jesus told them, 'I am the bread of life. Whoever comes to me will never become hungry, and whoever believes in me will never become thirsty.'" (John 6:35)

Lord, I am weary and my soul thirsts for you. I come to you in my weakness to partake of the bread of life and living water that I might have strength for this lonely journey. Lord, you are my strength.

Today's reading: Psalm 63

WEDNESDAY

"He placed a new song in my mouth, a song of praise to our God. He makes the path of life known to me." (Psalm 40:3, 16:11)

I know, Lord, that grief will come, but I have come to understand that everything has not been taken. You have shown me the path of eternal life and put a song in my heart that can never be taken away.

Today's reading: Psalm 150

THURSDAY

"Even though I walk into the middle of trouble, you guard my life against the anger of my enemies. O LORD, your mercy endures forever. Do not let go of what your hands have made." (Psalm 138:7,8)

When I venture into our troubled society, it bothers me so much, Lord, to see everyone going on their way as if nothing has happened when everything in my world has changed forever. Please don't let go of me.

Today's reading: Hebrews 13:5–21

FRIDAY

"In the world you'll have trouble. But cheer up! I have overcome the world." (John 16:33)

Though grief has cast its unwanted shadow on me, I know, Lord, that it comes to us all and is an inescapable part of life. Because of you, I do not grieve as those who have no hope, and I can overcome this pain and this loss.

Today's reading: 1 Thessalonians 4:13–18

Saturday

"Remember that I am always with you until the end of time, and I will never abandon you or leave you." (Matthew 28:20, Hebrews 13:5)

Thank you, Lord, that you died for me that I might live eternally. And for today, your Holy Spirit is here with me to comfort me and to remind me of all the things you have said. I need to hear you speak to me, Lord.

Today's reading: John 14

Week 14

S U N D A Y

"Lord, send your light and your truth. Let them guide me. Let them bring me to your holy mountain and to your dwelling place." (Psalm 43:3)

O Lord, I wish that I could be with you now in your dwelling place, free from the darkness that so often engulfs me. Bring me to your mountain and cause your face to shine upon me.

Today's reading: Psalm 43

M O N D A Y

"Teach me your way, O Lord, so that I may live in your truth. Focus my heart on fearing you." (Psalm 86:11)

There are so many thoughts that taunt me at times, that cause me to fear and doubt. Please, Lord, show me your way to live. Bring me into the knowledge of truth that my heart may be focused on you and you alone.

Today's reading: Proverbs 16

TUESDAY

"I am drowning in tears. Strengthen me as you promised. Graciously provide me with your teachings." (Psalm 119:28,29)

I can't sleep at night. I wake up crying. My sleep is no longer an escape. If you don't help me and come to my rescue, I will drown in my sorrow. I know there is a better way. Please teach me your word and strengthen me. Please renew my hope again.

Today's reading: 1 John 1

WEDNESDAY

"I have chosen a life of faithfulness. I have set your regulations in front of me. I have clung tightly to your written instructions. O LORD, do not let me be put to shame. I will eagerly pursue your commandments because you continue to increase my understanding." (Psalm 119:30–32)

I cling to every word that you have made real to me. Without your instructions, I would have no hope at all. Thank you for your word and for giving me more understanding every day. Please continue to strengthen me as I pursue your commands.

Today's reading: Proverbs 4

THURSDAY

*"Remember the word you gave me. Through it you gave me hope.
This is my comfort in my misery: Your promise gave me a new
life." (Psalm 119:49,50)*

It seems strange to me to be in so much sorrow and misery,
yet to have so much hope and life. I can't imagine facing this
trial without the hope and knowledge of you. Thank you for
giving me life.

Today's reading: Philippians 1

FRIDAY

*"Finally, brothers and sisters, keep your thoughts on whatever is
right or deserves praise: things that are true, honorable, fair, pure,
acceptable or commendable." (Philippians 4:8)*

When I remember the happy times we shared together, it
makes my grief a little lighter. There were so many happy
times and though this day was always a happy day, today is a
strange blend of happy memories and painful loss. Help me,
Lord, today, to think of those wonderful days and smile
through my tears.

Today's reading: Psalm 133

SATURDAY

"We, however, are citizens of heaven. We look forward to the Lord Jesus Christ coming from heaven as our Savior. Through his power to bring everything under his authority, he will change our humble bodies and make them like his glorified body." (Philippians 3:20,21)

One day, Lord! One glorious day, I will be changed in an instant, given a body that will never die, and reunited with those close to my heart who have departed this life before me. I now dream of streets of gold, but the one I love and miss so much walks daily upon them and will one day take my hand and show me their splendor.

Today's reading: Psalm 145

SUNDAY

"Because all people have sinned, they have fallen short of God's glory. Blessed are those whose disobedience is forgiven and whose sins are pardoned. Blessed is the person whom the Lord never considers sinful." (Romans 3:23, 4:7,8)

I know I have sinned and fallen short, but I am so thankful that when I depart this life, you welcome me as though I had never sinned. The one I now miss basks in your presence free from the condemnation and bondage of sin.

Today's reading: Psalm 71

MONDAY

"Therefore, the promise is based on faith so that it can be a gift, and the gift that God freely gives is everlasting life found in Christ Jesus our Lord." (Romans 4:16, 6:23)

What an unfathomable gift! The gift of life everlasting received by faith! Lord, you are so incredibly good to me. How much more in this time of grief I must rely on your promise and cling to its hope.

Today's reading: John 15

TUESDAY

"When there was nothing left to hope for, Abraham still hoped and believed. He didn't doubt God's promise out of a lack of faith, because he knew the one who made the promise was faithful." (Romans 4:18,20, Hebrews 10:23)

I know, like I never thought I would know, what it's like to have nothing left to hope for. Yet, like Abraham, somehow I still hope and trust with what's left of my battered faith that as you promised Lord, you are faithful and one day you will wipe away all my tears.

Today's reading: Hebrews 11

WEDNESDAY

"Never stop reciting these teachings. You must think about them night and day so that you will faithfully do everything written in them. Only then will you prosper and succeed." (Joshua 1:8)

Lord, to stop thinking about your teachings is not what worries me. I'm finding it a struggle just to get started. I am at times overwhelmed with thoughts about things which cannot be changed. Please help me, at times like these, to recall your kind instructions for life so that I may, in heart and soul both, prosper and succeed.

Today's reading: Psalm 102

THURSDAY

"I have commanded you, 'Be strong and courageous! Don't tremble or be terrified, because the Lord your God is with you wherever you go.'" (Joshua 1:9)

Lord, today I must go to the attorney's office and take care of business that I don't really understand. Only in you can I even hope to be strong, and in that hope I will muster all the courage I can to face the challenges of today. Thank you for going with me to this appointment.

Today's reading: Joshua 1

FRIDAY

"Lord God of heaven, great and awe-inspiring God, you faithfully keep your promise and show mercy to those who love you and obey your commandments. Open your eyes, and pay close attention with your ears to what I, your servant, am praying." (Nehemiah 1:5,6)

Thank you for your mercy today. It is so comforting to know that you always watch over me and listen to my prayers. I ask you now for grace to make it through another day.

Today's reading: Psalm 105

SATURDAY

"If you live by what I say, you are truly my disciples. You will know the truth, and the truth will set you free." (John 8:31,32)

Who else has the words of life? Where else can I turn? You alone, O God, have the words of life. You indeed are the way, the truth and the life. Lead me in your truth.

Today's reading: John 6

Week 16

SUNDAY

"We also brag when we are suffering. We know that suffering creates endurance, endurance creates character, and character creates confidence." (Romans 5:3,4)

I'm not there, Lord, but I'd like to be. If suffering brings character, then I know that as I learn to endure, your character and even your compassion will be formed in me. In the end, this experience will give me greater confidence and trust in your unfailing love.

Today's reading: Psalm 30

MONDAY

"I know that nothing good lives in me; that is, nothing good lives in my corrupt nature. Although I have the desire to do what is right, I don't do it. I don't do the good I want to do. Instead, I do the evil that I don't want to do." (Romans 7:18,19)

Father, at times I can all too readily agree with the Apostle Paul as I so easily identify with this statement. It seems I've tried everything to replace my loss. When will I learn that I can't replace my loss, only accept it?

Today's reading: Philippians 3

TUESDAY

"What a miserable person I am! Who will rescue me from my dying body? I thank God that our Lord Jesus Christ rescues me!" (Romans 7:24,25)

As I watch my own body slowly deteriorate, I remember how quickly came the loss of the one I loved so much. I take great comfort in knowing that when this body of mine is laid in the earth, you will rescue me from the grip of death.

Today's reading: Psalm 107

WEDNESDAY

"Those who are under the control of the corrupt nature can't please God. But if God's Spirit lives in you, you are under the control of your spiritual nature, not your corrupt nature." (Romans 8:8,9)

Thank you, Father, for placing your Holy Spirit in me. I don't want to be controlled by my corrupt nature, but rather by my spiritual nature which you have given me. Please help me to see what I'm going through now with spiritual eyes.

Today's reading: Acts 2

THURSDAY

"You haven't received the spirit of slaves that leads you into fear again. Instead, you have received the spirit of God's adopted children by which we call out, 'Abba! Father!' The Spirit himself testifies with our spirit that we are God's children." (Romans 8:15,16)

Father, remind me again that I am your child and that you are my loving Father, not some distant God. Please remind me again that you are as close as my breath, as near as my heart, and unfailing in your love for me.

Today's reading: Psalm 24

FRIDAY

"I consider our present sufferings insignificant compared to the glory that will soon be revealed to us. We groan as we eagerly wait for our adoption, the freeing of our bodies from sin." (Romans 8:18,23)

This present suffering shall pass as well, and when it does, it will fade into obscurity compared to the glory that I will then see. In the meantime, however, I find myself still groaning with the day-to-day agony of surviving a loneliness I didn't sign up for. Even so, come quickly, Lord Jesus!

Today's reading: Psalm 27

SATURDAY

"We know that all things work together for the good of those who love God—those whom he has called according to his plan."
(Romans 8:28)

Lord, I know this is true and I've seen it many times in the past, but right now I am struggling and cannot see the good that I know you can bring. Nevertheless, I thank you for calling me according to your plan and working for my good.

Today's reading: Isaiah 55

SUNDAY

"With perfect peace you will protect those whose minds cannot be changed, because they trust you. Trust the Lord always, because the Lord, the Lord alone, is an everlasting rock." (Isaiah 26:3,4)

Father, though the world and everything in it is a constant reminder of what I have lost, I can never forget or escape the wonderful truth that nothing is beyond your control. In that knowledge, I find peace.

Today's reading: Psalm 9

MONDAY

"The more words there are, the more pointless they become. What advantage do mortals gain from this?" (Ecclesiastes 6:11)

I know they mean well, Lord, but sometimes people say the most senseless things, and in doing so, they cause more harm than good. I don't need answers from them, just their friendship. In the meantime, Lord, thank you for always being a friend that sticks closer than a brother.

Today's reading: James 3

TUESDAY

"There is something being done on earth that is pointless. Righteous people suffer for what the wicked do, and wicked people get what the righteous deserve." (Ecclesiastes 8:14)

Even Solomon struggled with the apparent inequities of life, and I, who lack his wisdom, find contentment in knowing that in the end there is a day of reckoning. On that day all tears will be wiped away and the righteous will shine like the sun in your kingdom. I anxiously await that day!

Today's reading: Psalm 39

WEDNESDAY

"Trust the Lord with all your heart, and do not rely on your own understanding." (Proverbs 3:5)

Father, I can't rely on my own understanding because I simply have none with regards to this great loss. I am learning to live with unanswered questions and in doing so, faith grows, peace comes and joy knocks at the door.

Today's reading: 2 Kings 18

Week 17

THURSDAY

"A righteous person may fall seven times, but he gets up again. Don't laugh at me, my enemies. Although I've fallen, I will get up. Although I sit in the dark, the Lord is my light." (Proverbs 24:16, Micah 7:8)

Lord, I know a new day is coming, one in which I will once again stand strong. I know this is true because even though I feel such darkness around me, I am beginning to see the light. You, Lord, are my light.

Today's reading: John 8

FRIDAY

"Here is a poor man who called out. The Lord heard him and saved him from all his troubles. Taste and see that the Lord is good. Blessed is the person who takes refuge in him." (Psalm 34:6,8)

Save me, O Lord, from the troubles and grief that vex my soul. I take refuge in you today. I run to you and long to partake of your goodness. Show me afresh this goodness of yours and nourish my soul with it.

Today's Reading: Psalm 69

SATURDAY

"The Lord is near to those whose hearts are humble. He saves those whose spirits are crushed. The righteous person has many troubles, but the Lord rescues him from all of them." (Psalm 34:18,19)

Father, though my spirit has been crushed by the weight of this loss, my heart takes great comfort in your nearness. You have rescued me from many troubles but this surpasses them all. Please show yourself strong on my behalf.

Today's reading: Isaiah 45

Week 18

SUNDAY

"Arise! Shine! Your light has come, and the glory of the Lord has dawned. Darkness now covers the earth, and thick darkness covers the nations. But the Lord dawns, and his glory appears over you."
(Isaiah 60:1,2)

Today I long to feel your radiance. I know you are the light of the world. You have come and now live in me. There is so much darkness in the world, but you have come and brought light. Today, I will rise up and let your light shine through me.

Today's reading: John 9

MONDAY

*"Jerusalem has sinned so much that it has become a filthy thing ....
It gave no thought to its future. Its downfall was shocking."*
(Lamentations 1:8,9)

Father, I have waded through much sorrow of my past, barely giving thought to the future. Please draw my heart toward you and show me the bright future you have in store for my life. I don't want the thoughts of what I don't have to keep me from the reality of what you do have for me.

Today's reading: Jeremiah 17

TUESDAY

"I know the plans that I have for you, declares the Lord. They are plans for peace and not disaster, plans to give you a future filled with hope." (Jeremiah 29:11)

Just knowing that you have plans for me at all gives me hope. But to know your plans are for peace, and not disaster, creates in me an expectation of good things. No matter how bumpy the road down here, one day the path will be ever smooth.

Today's reading: Jeremiah 29

WEDNESDAY

"The ropes of death became tangled around me. The horrors of the grave took hold of me. When I was weak, he saved me. Be at peace again, my soul, because the Lord has been good to you." (Psalm 116:3,6,7)

Yes, death has its many ropes of sadness and despair, and they wrapped quickly around me. But now in my weakness, I find you slowly, carefully, unwinding those ropes and setting me free. My soul is finding peace as I watch you cut away the ropes of death. Thank you for your great kindness to me, Lord.

Today's reading: Psalm 6

THURSDAY

*"I will walk in the Lord's presence in this world of the living. I kept
my faith even when I said, 'I am suffering terribly.' How can I
repay the Lord for all the good that he has done for me?" (Psalm
116:9,10,12)*

Lord, the suffering I now endure will one day lighten. In the
meantime, while I walk among the living, I will remember all
the good you have done for me. My trust in you is not depend-
ent upon having a trouble-free life. I have kept my faith because you always bring me freedom in the midst of my trouble.

Today's reading: Hebrews 2

FRIDAY

*"Precious in the sight of the Lord is the death of his faithful ones."
(Psalm 116:15)*

Show me, Lord, how the loss of my loved one was precious or
costly in your sight. Give me a glimpse of how you felt. Show
me now what it is like for my loved one to be with you. Help
me come to grips with the reality of what I cannot see.

Today's reading: 2 Peter 1

SATURDAY

"At the same time the Spirit also helps us in our weakness, because we don't know how to pray for what we need. But the Spirit intercedes along with our groans that cannot be expressed in words. The one who searches our hearts knows what the Spirit has in mind. The Spirit intercedes for God's people the way God wants him to." (Romans 8:26,27)

Holy Spirit, please help me in my weakness. I'm not sure how to pray, but I do know a lot about groaning. I can't seem to find the words to express the tearing of my soul and my deep desire to be mended on the inside. Please pray for me.

Today's reading: Hebrews 7

Week 19

SUNDAY

"If God is for us, who can be against us? God didn't spare his own Son but handed him over to death for all of us. So he will also give us everything along with him." (Romans 8:31,32)

Father, you spared no expense for me. I can't imagine what it was like for you to willingly hand over your only son to die for me. Yet you did it. Now I know you understand and care deeply about my loss and will give me all that I need to come through it.

Today's reading: Psalm 3

MONDAY

"What will separate us from the love Christ has for us? Can trouble, distress, persecution, hunger, nakedness, danger, or violent death separate us from his love? I am convinced that nothing can ever separate us from God's love which Christ Jesus our Lord shows us." (Romans 8:35,38)

I am so grateful, Lord, that no pain, grief, or loss of any kind can ever separate me from your love. At times, I have isolated myself and felt quite alone. Then I remember your promise and take comfort in the knowledge that you are with me.

Today's reading: Hebrews 13

TUESDAY

"Always be joyful in the Lord! I'll say it again: Be joyful! Never worry about anything. But in every situation let God know what you need in prayers and requests while giving thanks. Then God's peace, which goes beyond anything we can imagine, will guard your thoughts and emotions through Christ Jesus." (Philippians 4:4,6)

I find it hard to be joyful when I am focusing on my loss. But when I focus on what I have gained in my relationship with you and the reward that will someday be mine, I find joy streaming into my heart. Lord, these days my soul is filled with both sunshine and rain, sometimes at the same time. But somehow in the mixture, I find peace. Thank you.

Today's reading: Psalm 11

WEDNESDAY

"I've learned to be content in whatever situation I'm in. I can do everything through Christ who strengthens me." (Philippians 4:11,13)

I am learning to be content in this, the most difficult time of my life. Yet I know as I spend time in your word, strength is infused within my soul, and what once I could not see, I now begin to see through the haze of my blurry eyes. What once I could not understand, I no longer seek to question. And in the wonder of it all, contentment comes.

Today's reading: Psalm 28

THURSDAY

"God has rescued us from the power of darkness and has brought us into the kingdom of his Son, whom he loves. His Son paid the price to free us, which means that our sins are forgiven."
(Colossians 1:13,14)

Not only have you rescued me from the power of spiritual darkness, but when one day my body is laid in a darkened grave, I will find myself free from death's grip, basking in the glorious light of your kingdom. Thank you for paying the price for my sins and forgiving me.

Today's reading: Psalm 17

FRIDAY

"We must also consider how to encourage each other to show love and to do good things. We should not stop gathering together with other believers, as some of you are doing. Instead, we must continue to encourage each other even more as we see the day of the Lord coming." (Hebrews 10:24,25)

Father, please use me today to encourage someone who needs to experience your love and your goodness. I'm not very strong yet, but I find as I reach out to others, something wonderfully soothing happens in me. I need some of that today.

Today's reading: Galatians 6

SATURDAY

"So don't lose your confidence. It will bring you a great reward. You need endurance so that after you have done what God wants you to do, you can receive what he has promised." (Hebrews 10:35,36)

I haven't lost my confidence, Lord, I'm just having a hard time finding it today. But I will find it because I have found you, and whenever I discover your nearness, my strength builds and my confidence reappears. I realize this process is building endurance in me so that I can complete the work you have for me and receive all that you have promised me.

Today's reading: Psalm 118

Week 20

SUNDAY

"The person who has God's approval will live because of faith. But if he turns back, I will not be pleased with him." (Hebrews 10:38)

You have given me your unconditional approval and because of that, I can now live by faith. Turning back is not an option, but pressing ahead is sometimes very difficult. Help me today as I take on new challenges and, by faith, venture into an uncertain future.

Today's reading: 1 Peter 4

MONDAY

"All people are like grass, and all their beauty is like a flower of the field. The grass dries up and the flower drops off, but the word of the Lord lasts forever." (1 Peter 1:24,25)

Help me, Lord, to grasp the fleeting nature of life in this realm. It seems like only yesterday I was with the one I now miss so much. Where did the time go? Why does it seem time spent passes like a lightning bolt, while time remaining in this life looms like a slow-moving storm cloud on a distant horizon? I take great courage, however, that no matter what changes in life, your word never does.

Today's reading: 2 Peter 3

TUESDAY

"I am laying a chosen and precious cornerstone in Zion, and the person who believes in him will never be ashamed. This honor belongs to those who believe." (1 Peter 2:6,7)

I believe in Christ Jesus with a sense of deliberateness and unashamedness that I have never known before. Before this tragedy struck, my walk with you, Lord, was all too often a walk of convenience. Now I am beginning to understand the honor it is to belong to you, and I thank you for that honor.

Today's reading: Ephesians 3

WEDNESDAY

"Dear friends, use your most holy faith to grow. Pray with the Holy Spirit's help. Remain in God's love as you look for the mercy of our Lord Jesus Christ to give you eternal life." (Jude 1:20,21)

By using my faith to grow, Lord, do you mean for me to step out and take some risks? I don't feel ready, but I am willing. Holy Spirit, please help me to pray, and lead me in the way I should go. Keep me in the love of God, and show me the mercy of our Lord Jesus Christ.

Today's reading: Philippians 2

Week 20

THURSDAY

"You alone created my inner being. You knitted me together inside my mother. I will give thanks to you because I have been so amazingly and miraculously made. Your works are miraculous, and my soul is fully aware of this." (Psalm 139: 13,14)

Lord, you know me from the inside out. You created me and formed me while I was inside my mother. You know what my limits are and have promised not to test me beyond what I am able to bear. I am amazed that I have been able to stand up to the test so far, even though I actually spent much of the time in a less than strong frame of mind.

Today's reading: 1 Corinthians 4

FRIDAY

"The Lord will bless you and watch over you. The Lord will smile on you and be kind to you. The Lord will look on you with favor and give you peace." (Numbers 6:24–26)

I close my eyes and imagine this blessing being prayed over me. Father, thank you for such a wonderful blessing found in your word, available to me. Give me favor in all my dealings today and flood my home with your peace.

Today's reading: Ephesians 1

SATURDAY

"How long, O Lord? Will you forget me forever? How long will you hide your face from me? How long must I make decisions alone with sorrow in my heart day after day? How long will my enemy triumph over me?" (Psalm 13:1,2)

I am so glad that I am not the only one who has ever felt that way. It amazes me that King David, a man after your own heart, actually penned these words. But thankfully you have not forgotten me, nor do I have to make decisions without the benefit of your counsel. Thank you, Lord, that the enemy of my soul no longer triumphs over me. Give me a fruitful day and please help me to continue lessening the sorrow in my heart.

Today's reading: 1 Thessalonians 1

Week 21

SUNDAY

"You are my hiding place. You protect me from trouble. You surround me with joyous songs of salvation." (Psalm 32:7)

It seems at times, Father, that life itself is not my friend, for I find myself assailed throughout the day with every kind of obstacle. But you are my hiding place, and as I draw near to you and bask in your presence, your love saves me from a spirit of oppression. I sing praises to you, Lord!

Today's reading: Psalm 34

MONDAY

"Our bodies are made of clay, yet we have the treasure of the Good News in them. This shows that the superior power of this treasure belongs to God and doesn't come from us." (2 Corinthians 4:7)

Every day I am reminded of my frailty, and though my body is made of clay, my spirit is eternal and belongs to you, Lord. Thank you for reclaiming me with the power of the treasured Good News, your glorious gospel, which saved me from the pit of despair.

Today's reading: 2 Corinthians 4

TUESDAY

"In every way we're troubled, but we aren't crushed by our troubles. We're frustrated, but we don't give up. We're persecuted, but we're not abandoned. We're captured, but we're not killed. We always carry around the death of Jesus in our bodies so that the life of Jesus is also shown in our bodies." (2 Corinthians 4:8–10)

I ran into some old friends who I hadn't seen for about a year. I knew they had heard about my loss, but when they greeted me, they never mentioned it or asked how I was doing. They just talked as though nothing had changed. Lord, I still need people to care, to ask, to show me love. Though I'm frustrated and feel somewhat abandoned, I don't give up. Thank you for placing your life in me.

Today's reading: Romans 15

WEDNESDAY

"The weapons we use in our fight are not made by humans. Rather, they are powerful weapons from God. With them we destroy people's defenses, that is, their arguments and all their intellectual arrogance that oppose the knowledge of God. We take every thought captive so that it is obedient to Christ." (2 Corinthians 10:4,5)

Week 21

Every day I fight a battle to not dwell on negative thoughts that will bring depression but instead to meditate on the TRUTH of God's word—Jesus Christ and life eternal.

Today's reading: John 14

THURSDAY

"In every situation let God know what you need in prayers and requests while giving thanks, for he hears the prayers of righteous people, and the prayers of decent people please him." (Philippians 4:6, Proverbs 15:29,15:8)

It means so much to know that you not only hear my prayers but that they actually please you. My friends have tired of my grief and urge me to "put it all behind me." That's like telling someone who has just had their right leg severed to "get over it!" Even when an amputee learns to walk again, he never forgets his loss and it is never totally "behind him." Thank you for giving me grace for my journey!

Today's reading: Hebrews 7

FRIDAY

"God is our refuge and strength, an ever-present help in times of trouble. Persecutions and sufferings will come, but the Lord rescued

me from all of them. Love never stops believing, never stops hoping, never gives up." (Psalm 46:1,2 Timothy 3:11, 1 Corinthians 13:7)

Lord, you promised that in this world we would have tribulation, and I know that in this fallen world we will have tragedy, death and sorrow. But we grieve, not as those who have no hope, for we have the hope that is in Christ alone. Thank you for that hope.

Today's reading: Hebrews 8 & 9

SATURDAY

"Finally, receive your power from the Lord and from his mighty strength. The LORD is my light and my salvation. Who is there to fear? Search for the Lord and his strength. Always seek his presence, and he will arm you with strength." (Ephesians 6:10, Psalm 27:1, 1 Chronicles 16:11, 2 Samuel 22:33)

Lord, I am so weak, but your strength is made perfect in weakness. Put your grace on me today that I may walk in your strength, fearing nothing. Today I will search for you and find your presence, that you may arm me with strength.

Today's reading: John 15 & 16

Week 22

SUNDAY

"My Messenger will go ahead of you. The Messenger of the LORD camps around those who fear him, and he rescues them. The Lord will go ahead of you, and smooth out the rough places. He will be with you. He won't abandon you or leave you. So don't be afraid or terrified. The battle isn't yours. It's God's." (Exodus 32:34, Psalm 34:7, Isaiah 45:2, Deuteronomy 31:8, 2 Chronicles 20:15)

Lord, I never get tired of reading how much you care about me and support me. This year has had more than its share of rough places—places I would never have chosen to go. Thank you for both going before me to smooth out the way and going with me to encourage me along this "trail of tears."

Today's reading: Psalm 126

MONDAY

"I can guarantee this truth: This is what will be done for someone who doesn't doubt but believes what he says will happen: He can say to this mountain, 'Be uprooted and thrown into the sea,' and it will be done for him." (Mark 11:23)

Father, as I look at my personal mountain of grief and its hardships, I realize two things: this mountain has limits, and it will be moved! Thank you for the victory in Christ Jesus. In this I take courage to face the day.

Today's reading: Mark 11

TUESDAY

"The Lord's eyes scan the whole world to find those whose hearts are committed to him and to strengthen them. Wait with hope for the Lord. Be strong, and let your heart be courageous. Yes, wait with hope for the Lord." (2 Chronicles 16:9, Psalm 27:14)

Though many questions go temporarily unanswered, my heart is unwaveringly committed to you, Lord. I wait on you now with expectant hope for strength and courage to live one day at a time.

Today's reading: Psalm 46

WEDNESDAY

"The righteous person has many troubles, but the Lord rescues him from all of them. The Lord is my rock and my fortress and my Savior, my God, my stronghold, my shield and the one in whom I take refuge. The righteous people cry out. The Lord hears and rescues them from all their troubles." (Psalm 34:19, 18:2, 144:2, 34:17)

When I'm weak, small troubles loom large, and large troubles seem unbearable. When I read your word, I am reminded that the righteous person has many troubles indeed, but you, Lord, deliver such a person out of them all, regardless of size. Today I ask you to rescue me from the troubles that wrap themselves around my neck like a hangman's noose. Set me free that I may worship you.

Today's reading: 1 Chronicles 16

THURSDAY

"It is better to depend on the Lord than to trust mortals, or influential people. I have taken refuge in you, O Lord. Never let me be put to shame." (Psalm 118:8,9; 31:1)

My trust is in you, Lord. I know that people will fail me, just as I fail others. This seems to be more a human condition than a malicious intent. In coming to you today, I ask that you help me make my words as reliable as yours, so that I never again cause shame due to a broken promise.

Today's reading: Psalm 25

FRIDAY

"Don't be afraid, because I am with you. Don't be intimidated; I am your God. I will strengthen you. I will help you. I will support you with my victorious right hand." (Isaiah 41:10)

Father, this loss has caused me to lose so much confidence. I'm trying to rebuild my confidence, and in the process I'm taking on small challenges to gain small victories. In the strength of your word and the knowledge that you are with me, I refuse to be intimidated. Grant me small victories today and bigger ones tomorrow.

Today's reading: 2 Timothy 1

SATURDAY

"God's way is perfect! The promise of the Lord has proven to be true. He is a shield to all those who take refuge in him. Besides, God will give you his constantly overflowing kindness. Then, when you always have everything you need, you can do more and more good things." (2 Samuel 22:31, 2 Corinthians 9:8)

I don't understand your ways, Lord, but I know they really are perfect. Your promises are always proven true and can always be counted on. You have, even in the midst of my complaining, continued to fill me with your kindness. Who else but you, Lord? And just think ... it is your intention to so fill me to overflowing that I will have everything I need so that I can do the good things you've planned for me to do.

Today's reading: 2 Corinthians 13

SUNDAY

"If you live by what I say, you are truly my disciples. You will know the truth, and the truth will set you free." (John 8:31,32)

Instruct my heart that I may know you. Show me how to live that I may both be your disciple and make disciples of others. Cause me to know you as I seek you, for in knowing you, I discover truth. Jesus, you are truth! In finding you, I find freedom. The bars of grief that would pen me in are being cut in half as freedom sounds its joyous song. Within my heart, a whisper is heard: "In a little while, my child."

Today's reading: Psalm 119

MONDAY

"Why are you discouraged, my soul? Why are you so restless? Put your hope in God, because I will still praise him. He is my savior and my God." (Psalm 42:5)

I cannot afford to remain in a constant state of depression, and I will not allow it. I will lift up my heavy heart and begin to praise you for all you have done for me. When I praise you, Lord, your presence becomes so real, and in your presence is fullness of joy.

Today's reading: Psalm 145

TUESDAY

"When you're in distress and all these things happen to you ... come back to the Lord your God and obey him, for if you are willing and obedient, you will eat the best from the land, and then you can confidently say, 'The Lord is my helper. I will not be afraid. What can mortals do to me?'" (Deuteronomy 4:30, Isaiah 1:19, Hebrews 13:6)

I turn to you in my distress and am both willing and obedient, desiring to once again enjoy some of the good things in life. Lord, it has been so long since I have felt like I "fit in" anywhere. Please start bringing me gently back into closer contact with the mainstream of society. Then with new found confidence, I, too, will say, "You are my help, what can mortals do to me?"

Today's reading: Psalm 143

WEDNESDAY

"My child, find your source of strength in the kindness of Christ Jesus. God in his kindness has given us his approval and we have become heirs who have the confidence that we have everlasting life." (2 Timothy 2:1, Titus 3:7)

In Christ alone I find my strength, and the kindness he has shown me is beyond comprehension. Father, thank you for such great love and compassion. Having your approval means everything to me and becoming an heir of everlasting life is a gift I can never repay.

Today's reading: Romans 10

THURSDAY

"Everything you say should be kind and well thought out so that you know how to answer everyone. That way the name of our Lord Jesus will be honored among you. Then, because of the good will of Jesus Christ, our God and Lord, you will be honored by him. Make sure that everyone has kindness from God so that bitterness doesn't take root and grow up to cause trouble that corrupts many of you." (Colossians 4:6, 2 Thessalonians 1:12, Hebrews 12:15)

I must admit, Lord, that bitterness has crept in, taken root and caused some trouble. My soul feels corrupted by it, and I need your grace to remove it and replace it with kindness. Give me grace and opportunity to repair damage I have done to any relationship. My pain has formed scabs over my wounds, becoming hard places in my soul that are cruel and unforgiving. Forgive me for my hard heartedness and please make me tender again.

Today's reading: Psalm 139

F R I D A Y

"You know the times in which we are living. It's time for you to wake up. Our salvation is nearer now than when we first became believers. The night is almost over, and the day is near." (Romans 13:11,12)

I still find myself wishing I could wake up and find out I've been having a long nightmare. I want to wake up and put this weight of grief off me, but it continues to enshroud me though it's been over five months now. I don't know when the night will be over, but I do know that the dawn is nearer now than when I first started down this lonely path.

Today's reading: Psalm 102

S A T U R D A Y

"We should get rid of the things that belong to the dark and take up weapons that belong to the light. We should live decently, as people who live in the light of day." (Romans 13:12,13)

Help me today, Lord, to get rid of attitudes that belong to the dark: thoughts that are destructive, aimed at holding me back and slowing my recovery. Your word is a shaft of light and a sword of truth. Give me the grace to lay hold of these weapons of light and the skill to use them on the forces of darkness.

Today's reading: Psalm 108

Week 24

SUNDAY

"A person's pride will humiliate him, for pride precedes a disaster, and an arrogant attitude precedes a fall. In fact, God opposes arrogant people, but he is kind to humble people, so be humbled by God's power so that when the right time comes he will honor you."
(Proverbs 29:23, 16:18, James 4:6, 1 Peter 5:6)

Lately I've been praying less and by doing so, implying that I can handle this on my own. Nothing could be further from the truth! Forgive me for walking in pride and not walking in dependence upon you. I humble myself now and ask for your kindness as I look for the day when I will be restored: body, soul and spirit.

Today's reading: Psalm 106

MONDAY

"Praise the Lord's greatness with me. Let us highly honor his name together, for he is the maker of heaven and earth, who says, 'Don't be afraid, because I am with you. Don't be intimidated; I am your God. I will strengthen you. I will help you. I will support you with my victorious right hand.'" (Psalm 34:3, 121:2, Isaiah 41:10)

As I praise and honor your name, magnifying you and making you bigger than all my problems, you give me strength and take away all my fears.

Today's reading: Isaiah 41

TUESDAY

"We have a chief priest who is able to sympathize with our weaknesses. He was tempted in every way that we are, but he didn't sin. So we can go confidently to the throne of God's kindness to receive mercy and find kindness, which will help us at the right time." (Hebrews 4:15,16)

When I am tempted to quit and give up this struggle, I remember your pain and suffering. Though tempted in every way, you endured without sin. I would like to be able to endure without sin, and so I approach your throne of kindness and ask for help in this, my time of need.

Today's reading: Hebrews 4 & 5

WEDNESDAY

"Let your mercy comfort me as you promised. Let my cry for help come into your presence, O Lord. Help me understand as you promised, for everything written long ago was written to teach us so that we would have confidence through the endurance and encouragement which the Scriptures give us." (Psalm 119:76,169, Romans 15:4)

I am greatly comforted by your mercy, and trust that my prayers are welcome in your presence. Give me confidence as I gain understanding and encouragement from the Scripture. As you guide me through your word and teach me your ways, renew my hope.

Today's reading: 1 Chronicles 16

THURSDAY

"I am worn out from my groaning. My eyes flood my bed every night. I soak my couch with tears. My eyes blur from grief."
(Psalm 6:6)

Lord, I still cry so easily. I can't hide my tears. When I am at home, I sob openly, yet it seems everyone wonders why I'm crying—everyone except those who have walked through this dark valley of grief and understand that grief keeps no one's schedule and has a language all its own. Those who have walked through grief, know its rhythm and understand its language. They know how to walk slowly with you and speak softly in unutterable words that sound more like quiet, yet reassuring, groans. Thank you for these people.

Today's reading: 1 Thessalonians 5

FRIDAY

"Open your ears to my words, O Lord. Consider my innermost thoughts. Pay attention to my cry for help, my king and my God, because I pray only to you." (Psalm 5:1,2)

Lord, only you know my innermost thoughts and the intentions of my heart. Sometimes when I pray, it's more with my heart than with my lips. It seems I can't get my lips to say what is in my heart without being disrupted by involuntary weeping. But do you know what, Lord? It seems that my tears actually release my pain and cleanse me from the "build up" of unresolved hurts. Thank you for the gift of tears.

Today's reading: Psalm 31

SATURDAY

"In the morning, O Lord, hear my voice. In the morning I lay my needs in front of you, and I wait." (Psalm 5:3)

Before I go out into the day, Lord, please show me what needs I should leave with you and which ones you want me to work on with your help today. I wait for you to lead me by your peace.

Today's reading: Psalm 25

Week 25

SUNDAY

"Don't love money. Be happy with what you have because God has said, 'I will never abandon you or leave you,' so trust him at all times, you people. Pour out your hearts in his presence. God is our refuge." (Hebrews 13:5, Psalm 62:8)

Father, I pour my heart out to you now and confess my sense of utter loneliness, even in the midst of friends and family, though they usually stay away because they are uncomfortable with my grief. I often feel alone and forgotten. But no matter what I feel, your word says that you'll never abandon me or leave me. I know your word is the truth. Thank you for being with me.

Today's reading: Psalm 32

MONDAY

"We must focus on Jesus, the source and goal of our faith. He saw the joy ahead of him, so he endured death on the cross and ignored the disgrace it brought him. Then he received the highest position in heaven, the one next to the throne of God. Think about Jesus, who endured opposition from sinners, so that you don't become tired and give up." (Hebrews 12:2,3)

When I think of all you gave up for me and all you endured so that I could live forever with you, I am breathless, without words.

Today's reading: 1 John 3

TUESDAY

"Those who cry while they plant will joyfully sing while they harvest. The person who goes out weeping, carrying his bag of seed, will come home singing, carrying his bundles of grain." (Psalm 126:5,6)

I'm weeping but I can't see my seed, for my seed has been laid in the ground and my grief waters it daily. On that great and wonderful day when the dead in Christ shall rise, I will see the fruit of my harvest and truly come home singing.

Today's reading: 1 Timothy 4

WEDNESDAY

"Weaklings should say that they are warriors." (Joel 3:10)

I feel like Gideon when he was asked to rescue Israel. He said his family was the weakest in Manasseh, and he was the least important member of the family. Lord, I can't rescue myself, let alone others, yet you tell me to say that I'm a warrior. If I can do all things through Christ, I guess I can say it: "I am a warrior." Armed with your word, protected by your blood, I am a warrior! Help me to war effectively against the enemy of my soul who constantly strives to knock me off my feet and kick me when I'm down.

Today's reading: Proverbs 18

THURSDAY

"Fear the Lord, you holy people who belong to him. Those who fear him are never in need. Young lions go hungry and may starve, but those who seek the Lord's help have all the good things they need." (Psalm 34:9,10)

There are so many who are much stronger than I right now, but you have promised to care for those who fear you regardless of their strength. Father, today I ask you for your help in regaining my enthusiasm for life. My times of weeping are somewhat intermittent, but in between I feel like a zombie. I would like to have a zest for life but feel guilty having that without the one whose loss I grieve. Help me to have your perspective on these things and not to be motivated by guilt.

Today's reading: Philippians 4:8

FRIDAY

"But God chose what the world considers nonsense to put wise people to shame. God chose what the world considers weak to put what is strong to shame. God chose what the world considers ordinary and what it despises—what it considers to be nothing—in order to destroy what it considers to be something." (1 Corinthians 1:27,28)

Many of my Christian friends who do not understand grief consider me to be weak, and many in the world think you should cut your losses and replace them as soon as possible. But I am finding that it takes strength to face grief and to walk through it, eventually emerging on the other side: healed—but still scarred; whole—but not complete; joyful—but not without sorrow. And when I emerge, by my example, I will destroy the myth of burying one's own pain.

Today's reading: Psalm 94

SATURDAY

"However, we have the mind of Christ." (1 Corinthians 2:16)

Lord, show me how in waiting on you, I can tap into your way of thinking, perceiving and understanding. Show me how to access your wisdom in times of decision. Help me grasp the seeds of truth as expressed in your written word and bring them to full harvest in my life.

Today's reading: Psalm 77

Week 26

SUNDAY

*"God's kingdom does not consist of what a person eats or drinks.
Rather, God's kingdom consists of God's approval and peace, as well
as the joy that the Holy Spirit gives. The person who serves Christ
with this in mind is pleasing to God and respected by people."*
(Romans 14:17,18)

So many people judge me by externals, as if to measure the
work of your kingdom within me. But your kingdom, Lord,
has more to do with your approval and that brings peace. The
resulting peace brings such unspeakable joy. I may never meet
the expectations of my fellow humans, but you have already
accepted and approved of me. How can I ever thank you?

Today's reading: Ephesians 2

MONDAY

*"If we live, we honor the Lord, and if we die, we honor the Lord.
So whether we live or die, we belong to the Lord. For this reason
Christ died and came back to life so that he would be the Lord of
both the living and the dead." (Romans 14:8,9)*

I am so glad that I belong to you! Whether I live or die, either
way, I'm yours! What a comfort! Especially as I think of the
one whose loss I grieve every day. You experienced death and
came back to life just to make me yours. You knew the pain

that death would cause, so you purchased me with your blood and became Lord of both the living and the dead. Thank you!

Today's reading: Romans 14

TUESDAY
"Brothers and sisters, I couldn't talk to you as spiritual people but as people still influenced by your corrupt nature." (1 Corinthians 3:1)

I used to think I was so spiritually mature, then my world caved in! I began to wonder if I even belonged to you. My grief, compounded with a sense of baseless guilt, drove me to very lonely places where my corrupt nature showed its face. I discovered that I could do little more than to cling to you, Lord, and trust in your mercy and wait for your grace.

Today's reading: 1 Peter 2

WEDNESDAY
"Everyone who hears what I say but doesn't obey it will be like a foolish person who built a house on sand. Rain poured, and floods came. Winds blew and struck that house. It collapsed, and the result was a total disaster." (Matthew 7:26,27)

When the storms of life come our way, we find out what in our life is built on sand and what is built on a sure rock foundation. This loss, though so unwanted, has shown me many faulty assumptions I had about you and your word. At the same time, it has shown me that when the storm clouds moved past, my relationship with you was still very much intact.

Today's reading: Matthew 7

THURSDAY

"Whenever you pray, forgive anything you have against anyone. Then your Father in heaven will forgive your failures." (Mark 11:25)

Someone told me that if I had just had more faith, I wouldn't have had to suffer this loss. Father, I don't know how to deal with such unkind, unthinking people who think they are "speaking the truth in love." I can only forgive them in Jesus' name and pray they will never have to go through a similar crisis.

Today's reading: Matthew 12

FRIDAY

"They eat with you and don't feel ashamed. They are shepherds who care only for themselves. They are dry clouds blown around by the winds. They are withered, uprooted trees without any fruit." (Jude 1:12)

It's been nearly six months since the funeral. So many people came, and I was deeply touched by their expression of love. It's also been nearly six months since I've heard from any of them, except one or two. "If there's anything you need, just call me," they said. Don't they know what I need is for them to call me?

Today's reading: Isaiah 49

SATURDAY

"I fall asleep in peace the moment I lie down because you alone, O Lord, enable me to live securely." (Psalm 4:8)

Father, please give me sleep like that. When I eventually do fall asleep, I wake up several times during the night. Something of my secure world was snatched away and I haven't felt as secure since then. Please reestablish my sense of security and help me to place all my confidence and trust in you.

Today's reading: Psalm 127

Week 27

SUNDAY

"May the words from my mouth and the thoughts from my heart be acceptable to you, O Lord, my rock and my defender." (Psalm 19:14)

Lord, all too often I spend time entertaining fearful thoughts and speaking negative words. You are my rock and my defender. What can people do to me? When my thoughts drift to barren places, please speak gently to my soul and remind me of your presence.

Today's reading: Ephesians 4

MONDAY

"The Lord is near to those whose hearts are humble. He saves those whose spirits are crushed." (Psalm 34:18)

Father, I humble myself in your presence, freely admitting my great need for your love, your assistance and oftentimes, your emergency rescue. My spirits have been crushed like grapes in a winepress. Can you turn these grapes into wine? Can you make me a better person after all of this? Please save me from my self-destructive thoughts.

Today's reading: Isaiah 42

TUESDAY

"Countless evils have surrounded me. My sins have caught up with me so that I can no longer see. They outnumber the hairs on my head. I have lost heart." (Psalm 40:12)

Father, it seems that when I want to do what is right, I find myself locked in self-defeating behavior patterns. I sin, I repent, and I do the same thing over again until I have just about lost heart. Please deliver me from the sin which so easily trips me up.

Today's reading: Hebrews 12

WEDNESDAY

"Create a clean heart in me, O God, and renew a faithful spirit within me. Do not force me away from your presence, and do not take your Holy Spirit from me. Restore the joy of your salvation to me, and provide me with a spirit of willing obedience." (Psalm 51:10–12)

Faithfulness, O Lord, is what I ask you to cultivate in me. I am having such a hard time being faithful in ordinary tasks. I lose interest quickly and turn to something else. Renew faithfulness in me towards you, my family, other relationships, my gifts and my responsibilities. Bring back the joy of my salvation and stimulate faithfulness in me.

Today's reading: Psalm 143

THURSDAY

"Focus my heart on fearing you. I will give thanks to you with all my heart, O Lord my God. I will honor you forever because your mercy toward me is great. You have rescued me from the depths of hell." (Psalm 86:11–13)

Lord, when I try to focus my thoughts on you by spending time in your word or reading uplifting materials, I find my mind drifts. I often get to the bottom of the page and realize I have no idea what I've just read. I want to honor you with my whole heart because you have rescued me from the depths of hell, but I am having a hard time concentrating. Please help me to focus my heart on you.

Today's reading: Psalm 146

FRIDAY

"Careless words stab like a sword, but the words of wise people bring healing." (Proverbs 12:18)

Why do those who have never suffered a devastating loss find it so easy to speak careless words that cut to the heart? I know they mean well, Lord, but please bring wise people into my life who have walked this path before me and can encourage me as I take this journey into uncharted waters.

Today's reading: Proverbs 10

SATURDAY

"Jesus asked, 'What is the kingdom of God like? What can I compare it to? It's like a mustard seed that someone planted in a garden. It grew and became a tree, and the birds nested in its branches.'"
(Luke 13:18,19)

Sometimes I feel like a mustard seed—small and insignificant. Plant me, Lord, in your garden and cause me to grow into something purposeful. Surely the potential you put in me is not less than you put in a mere seed. Help me to discover the potential you placed in me and bring me to my destiny.

Today's reading: Luke 12

Week 28

SUNDAY

*"If any of you needs wisdom to know what you should do, you
should ask God, and he will give it to you. God is generous to
everyone and doesn't find fault with them." (James 1:5)*

For too long, Lord, I thought of you as a distant, impersonal
God who had good reason to find fault with me. Then I started reading your word instead of listening to the accusing
words of ignorant people. I found a kind and generous God
ready to forgive, quick to answer and very, very personal.
Thank you for inviting me to come to ask you for wisdom
anytime. Grant me wisdom today, Lord.

Today's reading: Psalm 111

MONDAY

*"When you ask for something, don't have any doubts. A person
who has doubts is like a wave that is blown by the wind and tossed
by the sea. A person who has doubts shouldn't expect to receive
anything from the Lord. A person who has doubts is thinking about
two different things at the same time and can't make up his mind
about anything." (James 1:6–8)*

Father, admittedly I have wavered between two opinions on
many issues. Should I sell? Should I move? Should I do this
or that? I am beginning to think that my wavering is a good

indication of low stability and that I should not make any life changing decisions at this point. I do ask you to settle my mind, establish my heart and calm my troubled soul so I can discern your wisdom and make sound decisions.

Today's reading: Luke 8

TUESDAY

"Faith assures us of things we expect and convinces us of the existence of things we cannot see. Give us more faith." (Hebrews 11:1, Luke 17:5)

Yesterday, I saw someone who looked just like the one whose loss I grieve every day. For a moment I thought, "Could it be?" Then the person turned in my direction and dashed my foolish notion. This happens often, Lord, though not as often as it used to, and when it does, I draw on the assurance that one day my loved one and I will see each other again in a place free from pain and sorrow.

Today's reading: Galatians 3

WEDNESDAY

"Jesus told his disciples, 'Situations that cause people to lose their faith are certain to arise. But how horrible it will be for the person who causes someone to lose his faith!'" (Luke 17:1)

Sometimes people ask me if I'm mad at you, Lord. They are sure my faith must have really been tested with this loss. I know others have suffered similar losses and temporarily lost their faith and even blamed you. But you are the only one giving me hope, and to that hope I cling. Please show yourself strong on my behalf today.

Today's reading: Luke 9

THURSDAY

"As high as the heavens are above the earth—that is how vast his mercy is toward those who fear him. As far as the east is from the west—that is how far he has removed our rebellious acts from himself." (Psalm 103:11,12)

I've heard it said that mercy is "not getting what you do deserve: judgment" and grace is "getting what you don't deserve: kindness." I know I've done nothing worthy of eternal life, yet you purchased it for me anyway with your own blood. Your kindness and mercy know no limits.

Today's reading: Romans 2

FRIDAY

"The Lord will continually guide you and satisfy you even in sun-baked places. He will strengthen your bones. You will become like a watered garden and like a spring whose water does not stop flowing." (Isaiah 58:11)

I feel like I'm in a sun-baked place where cool, refreshing springs are few and far between. It seems so long since I've really laughed and let my guard down. Strengthen me today. Make me like a spring whose water does not stop flowing. Restore me to a place where I can be of encouragement to others. Please guide me in my thoughts today.

Today's reading: Proverbs 17:22

SATURDAY

"I find joy in your promise like someone who finds a priceless treasure." (Psalm 119:162)

Where would I be without your promises? They sustain me from day to day. Your word is your bond and everything you say can be counted on. When I think on these things, my heart is joyful and for a fleeting moment, I see the bright rays of a new day approaching. Thank you for your promises.

Today's reading: Psalm 119:105

Week 29

SUNDAY

"By the rivers of Babylon, we sat down and cried as we remembered Zion." (Psalm 137:1)

Lord, there are so many things that remind me of my loss. Every time I see a certain kind of car or drive past a certain place, memories flood my mind and flow down my cheeks as tears. Why is it that so many things bring back such strong memories? I'm not sure why, but when it happens, when I remember what used to be and what could have been, I become acutely aware of what is no longer, and I take refuge in you.

Today's reading: Psalm 48

MONDAY

"This is the day the Lord has made. Let's rejoice and be glad today, because the joy you have in the Lord is your strength. In fact, we should always bring God a sacrifice of praise, that is, words that acknowledge him." (Psalm 118:24, Nehemiah 8:10, Hebrews 13:15)

Lord, you have made this day with all of its glory. You have clothed the grass with flowers and filled the streams with life. You have caused the sun to shine even when I can't always see it. I will give thanks to you today for the many things you have done for me. I will offer up a sacrifice of praise and acknowledge you with my words. I will draw strength from you as your joy fills my soul.

Today's reading: Nehemiah 8

TUESDAY

"Consider this: The Father has given us his love. He loves us so much that we are actually called God's dear children. And that's what we are. For this reason the world doesn't recognize us, and it didn't recognize him either." (1 John 3:1)

I think of how much I love my own children and am taken aback to think that you love me even more. All too often I perceive myself as a lowly subject in your kingdom instead of a dear child in your family. Please help me to accept the fact that you love me as your own, and in giving your only Son, you would hold no good thing back from me.

Today's reading: John 1

WEDNESDAY

"God was also pleased to bring everything on earth and in heaven back to himself through Christ. He did this by making peace through Christ's blood sacrificed on the cross. So he is our peace—having been crushed for our sins and punished so that we could have peace." (Colossians 1:20, Ephesians 2:14, Isaiah 53:5)

I am so amazed that you took the punishment that I deserved, Lord. You wanted to reconcile your children to yourself, and you stopped at nothing to do this. What a price! I purpose today to cultivate a heart of gratitude, remembering what you did for me. As I do that, it seems that my greatest loss, though still painful, pales in comparison with the price you paid for me. Thank you for being my peace.

Today's reading: John 17

THURSDAY

"The Lord is my shepherd. I am never in need. He makes me lie down in green pastures. He leads me beside peaceful waters. He renews my soul. He guides me along the paths of righteousness for the sake of his name." (Psalm 23:1–3)

Lord, you have slowed down the pace of my life, and in doing so, you have given me more time to discover you again and to find my faith which at times seemed more like a memory than a current reality. I am beginning to be at peace with certain unalterable facts, though I still need you to tell me that everything is going to be all right. Thank you for working within me.

Today's reading: John 12

FRIDAY

"The Spirit of the Almighty Lord is with me because the Lord has anoint-ed me to deliver good news to humble people. He has sent me to heal those who are brokenhearted, to announce that captives will be set free and prisoners will be released." (Isaiah 61:1)

Lord, you came to heal the brokenhearted and set captives free. After all these months, I am noticing a subtle renewal or restoration within me, and I think I'm beginning to heal. Strangely, I feel some-how guilty about this, as though I'm being disloyal. I want to move forward, but there is a strange emotional pull fighting to keep me where I am. I'm confused. Please set me free from the battle within.

Today's reading: Psalm 10

SATURDAY

"...Rather, what matters is being a new creation." (Galatians 6:15)

When the one I loved died, a part of me died also. I feel like a cater-pillar fresh out of the cocoon. I'm not where I used to be and I'm not where I'm going. I'm just someplace in between a cocoon and a butterfly, crawling haltingly through unfamiliar territory, gazing ner-vously at my destiny while still recovering from my past. Lord, I don't feel ready to be a butterfly, but I think the process has started. Please help.

Today's reading: 2 Corinthians 9

Week 30

SUNDAY

"A thief comes to steal, kill and destroy. But I came so that my sheep will have life and so that they will have everything they need. I am the good shepherd. The good shepherd gives his life for the sheep." (John 10:10,11)

Sometimes, Lord, in the middle of my day, thoughts come that steal my frail happiness and destroy my sense of peace. Enable me to rise above the clouds of gloom that come uninvited to my life. You gave your life so that I could have life in abundance. Truly, you are the good shepherd.

Today's reading: Psalm 65

MONDAY

"Not everyone who says to me, 'Lord, Lord!' will enter the kingdom of heaven, but only the person who does what my Father in heaven wants." (Matthew 7:21)

Show me your will today, Father. Make it clear what you would like me to do, and I will do it. I am grateful that I have the desire again to be of service to you. You have done so much for me, how can I do anything less?

Today's reading: Psalm 97

TUESDAY

"Christ paid the price so that the blessing promised to Abraham would come to all the people of the world through Jesus Christ and we would receive the promised Spirit through faith." (Galatians 3:14)

Thank you, Lord, for paying the price so that the blessing promised to Abraham could be mine. I receive your Spirit by faith and know that he will lead me and teach me all things concerning you. Holy Spirit, you are the blessed Comforter. Thank you for comforting me in my difficult times.

Today's reading: Luke 11

WEDNESDAY

"Can a woman forget her nursing child? Will she have no compassion on the child from her womb? Although mothers may forget, I will not forget you. I have engraved you on the palms of my hands. Your walls are always in my presence." (Isaiah 49:15,16)

I feel like everyone has forgotten what happened and how it changed my life forever, but I am greatly comforted knowing that no matter who on earth has forgotten, you have not! You said you have engraved me on your hands. Is that what the nail prints signify?

Today's reading: Isaiah 53

THURSDAY

"This is what the Lord, your Defender, the Holy One of Israel, says: 'I am the Lord your God. I teach you what is best for you. I lead you where you should go.'" (Isaiah 48:17)

Lord, my heart is an open book. Please teach me how to grow from the painful hurts of life. Help me to accept what cannot be changed and to gain strength and character from this loss. Lead me today in the way I should go, guiding me into all that you have planned for me.

Today's reading: Isaiah 48

FRIDAY

"'I have refined you, but not like silver. I have tested you in the furnace of suffering.' Faith knows the power that his coming back to life gives and what it means to share his suffering. In this way I'm becoming like him in his death, with the confidence that I'll come back to life from the dead." (Isaiah 48:10, Philippians 3:10–11)

Lord, I feel very much like I have been in the furnace for the last seven months, yet I know my suffering cannot compare with the suffering you endured on the cross for me. As I walk through this discomfort, I feel a little closer to you, knowing what you endured. In the process, please make me more like you.

Today's reading: Psalm 66

SATURDAY

"It's not that I've already reached the goal or have already completed the course. But I run to win that which Jesus Christ has already won for me. Brothers and sisters, I can't consider myself a winner yet. This is what I do: I don't look back, I lengthen my stride, and I run straight toward the goal to win the prize that God's heavenly call offers in Christ Jesus." (Philippians 3:12–14)

I know I haven't reached the goal yet, but Lord, I want to have everything you won for me. You certainly won my eternal salvation and that I receive with great gratitude. Help me to avoid looking back and to press forward and fulfill my destiny.

Today's reading: Matthew 25

Week 31

"So those who are believers in Christ Jesus can no longer be con-
demned. The standards of the Spirit, who gives life through Christ
Jesus, have set you free from the standards of sin and death."
(Romans 8:1,2)

Free from condemnation! Lord, I could never live up to your
standards because of my own weakness, but you came with a
human nature and paid the price for me. Now I am free to
live by the spiritual nature you have given me. Show me how
to live that life the way you intended.

Today's reading: Romans 6

M O N D A Y

"Job stood up, tore his robe in grief, and shaved his head. Then he
fell to the ground and worshiped. He said 'Naked I came from my
mother, and naked I will return. The Lord has given, and the Lord
has taken away! May the name of the Lord be praised.' Through
all this Job did not sin or blame God for doing anything wrong."
(Job 1:20–22)

I came into this world with nothing, and it is certain I will
leave with nothing. All that is in this temporal realm, that I
think I own, will all be passed on to someone else. Ultimately
Lord, you own it all. I just get to use things for awhile. Help

me to recognize your ownership in all things and to glorify you in my use of them. May your name be praised in all the earth.

Today's reading: Psalm 50

TUESDAY

"The Lord your God is with you. He is a hero who saves you. He happily rejoices over you, renews you with his love, and celebrates over you with shouts of joy." (Zephaniah 3:17)

Lord, it is so hard for me to imagine that you love me this much. Forgive my foolish and doubting heart! I should have known that if you would humble yourself to come as a man, even a servant, suffer cruel punishment and die on a cross for me, that you would also renew me with your love and celebrate over me with shouts of joy.

Today's reading: Zephaniah 3

WEDNESDAY

"In the last days the mountain of the Lord's house will be established as the highest of the mountains and raised above the hills. People will stream to it. Then many nations will come and say, 'Let's go to the mountain of the Lord, to the house of the God of

Jacob. He will teach us his ways so that we may live by them.'"
(Micah 4:1,2)

I long for that day, Lord, when the nations will come and
desire to learn about you. Even now I yearn to know your
ways so that I can truly live by them. Father, so many things
became unclear when I suffered that loss. Please help me to
regain clarity and understanding on vital issues concerning
life itself.

Today's reading: 2 Timothy 3

THURSDAY
*"Hammer your plow blades into swords and your pruning shears
into spears. Weaklings should say that they are warriors. The Lord
will roar from Zion, and his voice will thunder from Jerusalem. The
sky and the earth will shake. The Lord will be a refuge for his people. He will be a stronghold for the people of Israel." (Joel 3:10,16)*

Lord, you are increasing my strength and building my confidence. I know that when I step out to accomplish something,
you will go with me. If the task overwhelms me, you will be
my refuge.

Today's reading: Proverbs 14

FRIDAY

"Israel, I will make you my wife forever. I will be honest and faithful to you. I will show you my love and compassion. I will be true to you, my wife. Then you will know the Lord." (Hosea 2:19,20)

Lord, you go to such lengths to help me understand your love for me and your commitment to me! Show me your love and compassion afresh so that I may know you more intimately and respond to you in love.

Today's reading: Psalm 89

SATURDAY

"The secret was revealed to Daniel in a vision during the night. So Daniel praised the God of heaven." (Daniel 2:19)

Lord, I can't tell you how many nights I have wanted to dream and see again the face of the one I love. If I could only get a glimpse of what life is like for my loved one now, I would be eternally grateful. Nevertheless, I trust you for what is best for me now and leave that request in your hands.

Today's reading: Psalm 62

Week 32

SUNDAY

"Son of man, all the people of Israel are like these bones. The people say, 'Our bones are dry, and our hope is vanished. We are completely destroyed.' So prophesy. Tell them, 'This is what the Almighty Lord says: My people, I will open your graves and take you out of them. I will bring you to Israel. Then, my people, you will know that I am the Lord, because I will open your graves and bring you out of your graves. I will put my Spirit in you, and you will live.'" (Ezekiel 37:11–14)

So many times, Lord, I have felt like my spirit was dry and my hope had vanished. The loss I felt held me in its own grave. Then you came by your Spirit and lifted me, gently separating me from the deathly pull of my loss. Thank you for putting your Spirit within me.

Today's reading: Psalm 3

MONDAY

"Cursed is the person who trusts humans, who makes flesh and blood his strength and whose heart turns away from the Lord. He will be like a bush in the wilderness. He will not see when something good comes. He will live in the dry places in the desert, in a salty land where no one can live." (Jeremiah 17:5,6)

I will not put my trust in people or my confidence in what insurance companies promise, nor will I allow my heart to turn away from you, my Lord. If I'm looking at others for my provision, I will certainly miss the good that comes from your hand. I've been living in dry places long enough, and I am ready for you to show yourself strong on my behalf.

Today's reading: Psalm 78

TUESDAY

"Blessed is the person who trusts the Lord. The Lord will be his confidence. He will be like a tree that is planted by water. It will send its roots down to a stream. It will not be afraid in the heat of summer. Its leaves will turn green. It will not be anxious during droughts. It will not stop producing fruit." (Jeremiah 17:7,8)

Indeed, you are my confidence, Lord, as I earnestly place all my trust in you. Make me like the tree that reaches deep down and draws on the living waters for sustenance. Your Spirit in me is the stream of living water that gives me the grace to endure the heat of affliction and to face down the fear of drought. Make me fruitful again, Lord, and so firmly establish me in you that I never again stop being fruitful.

Today's reading: John 4

WEDNESDAY

"The human mind is the most deceitful of all things. It is incurable. No one can understand how deceitful it is. I, the Lord, search minds and test hearts. I will reward each person for what he has done. I will reward him for the results of his actions." (Jeremiah 17:9,10)

Search my heart and mind, Lord, and expose my deceitful ways. Create a clean heart for me, and renew a right spirit within me. Show me the works you have for me, so on that day you can say to me, "Well done, good and faithful servant."

Today's reading: Jeremiah 17

THURSDAY

"I am the Lord, and there is no other. I make light and create darkness. I make blessings and create disasters. I, the Lord, do all these things." (Isaiah 45:6,7)

Lord, the more I know you, the more I realize how little I know you. Certainly, there is none like you!

Today's reading: Matthew 4

FRIDAY

"My thoughts are not your thoughts, and my ways are not your ways, declares the Lord. Just as the heavens are higher than the earth, so my ways are higher than your ways, and my thoughts are higher than your thoughts." (Isaiah 55:8,9)

Lord, take me into the realm of your thoughts and show me a glimpse of your wisdom, if my mind can handle it. Teach me to think like you think and to walk in your ways. I want to touch that higher way of living and help others to do the same.

Today's reading: 2 Chronicles 1

SATURDAY

"Call to me, and I will answer you. I will tell you great and mysterious things that you do not know. I, Wisdom, live with insight, and I acquire knowledge and foresight, and the Lord has reserved this priceless wisdom for decent people." (Jeremiah 33:3, Proverbs 8:12, 2:7)

Lord, I'm calling out to you, asking you to tell me great and mysterious things that I do not know. Share with me your wisdom, knowledge and foresight. Grant me insight for living as I prepare my heart for a future I cannot see.

Today's reading: Isaiah 11

SUNDAY

"Honor the Lord with your wealth and with the first and best part of all your income. Then your barns will be full, and your vats will overflow with fresh wine." (Proverbs 3:9,10)

Father, as I begin this week, show me how to honor you with what you have given me. I'm coming to understand that you have placed great wealth within me. Show me how to honor you with that wealth—those talents—that my life may be full and complete again in you.

Today's reading: Malachi 3

MONDAY

"The first servant said, 'Sir, the coin you gave me has earned ten times as much.' The king said to him, 'Good job! You're a good servant. You proved that you could be trusted with a little money. Take charge of ten cities.'" (Luke 19:16,17)

One day, Lord, you are going to ask me to give an account of my life and what I did with what you gave me. Although I suffered a tremendous loss nearly eight months ago which took away my zest for life and robbed me of my fruitfulness, I want to get on my feet again and back in the game of life. I still feel very fragile, but I'm trusting you for my future.

Today's reading: John 5

TUESDAY

"A joyful heart is good medicine, but depression drains one's strength." (Proverbs 17:22)

For so long, my strength has been drained by the depression that lurks beneath the surface of my consciousness. I'm always just a teardrop away from a flood of depression. I think I'm handling it fine, then the slightest little thing will anger me. I lose sleep and I can't concentrate on my work. I wonder, will the pain ever leave me alone? Lord, I need some of that joyful medicine if I'm ever going to make it through this.

Today's reading: Psalm 100

WEDNESDAY

"The crucible is for refining silver and the smelter for gold, but the one who purifies hearts by fire is the Lord." (Proverbs 17:3)

Lord, in all of this process I ask that you purify my heart and conform me to your likeness. Remove the dross and all that would hinder me from serving you. Strengthen me, test me, then strengthen me again. Yes break me, bless me and send me to the world. Make my life count for you, Lord.

Today's reading: Isaiah 30

THURSDAY

"Pay attention to yourselves and to the entire flock in which the Holy Spirit has placed you as bishops to be shepherds for God's church which he acquired with his own blood." (Acts 20:28)

Lord, you have purchased me with your own blood. I belong to you. Spend what's left of my life in any way that you see fit. So much has changed in the last year, so many dreams have been dashed, so many plans lie in ruin. I don't know where to go from here, so I offer you my life and ask you to make the most of it for your glory.

Today's reading: 1 Corinthians 6

FRIDAY

"But Jesus called the infants to him and said, 'Don't stop the children from coming to me! Children like these are part of the kingdom of God. I can guarantee this truth: Whoever doesn't receive the kingdom of God as a little child receives it will never enter it.'" (Luke 18:16,17)

Renew childlike faith in me, Lord. Help me to trust you simply at your word. Enable me to laugh at little things, find pleasure in simple obedience and be joyful in all things.

Today's reading: Psalm 112

SATURDAY

"He divided the sea and led them through it. He made the waters stand up like a wall. He guided them by a cloud during the day and by a fiery light throughout the night. He split rocks in the desert. He gave them plenty to drink, an ocean of water. He made streams come out of a rock. He made the water flow like rivers."
(Psalm 78:13–16)

Lord, there is nothing too hard for you. If you could make water come out of a rock, you can renew my spirit again. If you could satisfy the natural thirst of a rebellious people, I know you can satisfy my longing for spiritual life again. If you could guide with fire and clouds, surely you can lead me through these difficult times. I commit my life into your hands and ask you Lord to cause your Spirit to flow out of me like rivers of living water.

Today's reading: John 7

Week 34

SUNDAY

"Do not be afraid, because I have reclaimed you. I have called you by name; you are mine. When you go through the sea, I am with you. When you go through rivers, they will not sweep you away. When you walk through fire, you will not be burned, and the flames will not harm you." (Isaiah 43:1,2)

Father, before this loss I had no idea what a vast expanse this grief would be. I feel like I've been swimming in an ocean of grief with no shore in sight. Every time I think I've spotted land on the horizon, it is another storm cloud forming. What makes it possible for me to endure is the knowledge that you are with me and will keep me from drowning in my own sorrow.

Today's reading: Psalm 121

MONDAY

"Moses said to them, 'Why are you complaining to me? Why are you testing the Lord?' But the people were thirsty for water there. They complained to Moses and asked, 'Why did you bring us out of Egypt? Was it to make us, our children, and our livestock die of thirst?' They will know that I am the Lord their God. I brought them out of Egypt so that I might live among them. I am the Lord their God." (Exodus 17:2,3, 29:46)

Lord, how many times have I, like the children of Israel, misunderstood and wrongly judged you? You wanted a people of your own, called by your name for you to live among. You wanted to be their God and to supply their needs. When the harshness of my circumstances exceeded the tenderness of my heart, I have blamed and complained. Please forgive me, Lord. Live with me and be my God.

Today's reading: Jeremiah 31

TUESDAY

"Moses answered the people, 'Don't be afraid! Stand still, and see what the Lord will do to save you today. You will never see these Egyptians again. The Lord is fighting for you! So be still!'"
(Exodus 14:13,14)

How many times have you been fighting for me when I did not know it? There have been plenty of times that you have fought for me when I did know it, but I'm sure there have been many more that I didn't know. I am learning to be still and know that you are doing things for me of which I have never even dreamed.

Today's reading: Psalm 130

WEDNESDAY

"I, the Lord, have called you to do what is right. I will take hold of your hand. I will protect you. I will appoint you as my promise to the people, as my light to the nations." (Isaiah 42:6)

I am stepping out, purposing to do the right thing, Father. I need to know that your hand is there for me to hold and that you will protect me. Although you have appointed me to be a light in this world, I'm running on very low voltage right now. Please recharge my batteries and help me to be all that you intend.

Today's reading: Psalm 19

THURSDAY

"He will not break off a damaged cattail. He will not even put out a smoking wick. He will not be discouraged or crushed until he has set up justice on the earth." (Isaiah 42:3,4)

I sometimes feel like a limp, damaged cattail, barely able to remain standing. I rejoice to discover that you don't discard the wounded. At other times I feel like a candle whose light has gone out, leaving only smoke as a silent reminder of what once was. What an encouragement to know that you will not snuff out the candle, though it has temporarily lost its flame.

Today's reading: Psalm 136

FRIDAY

"'You are my witnesses,' declares the Lord. 'I have chosen you as my servant so that you can know and believe in me and understand that I am the one who did this. No god was formed before me, and there will be none after me. I alone am the Lord, and there is no savior except me.'" (Isaiah 43:10,11)

Thank you for choosing me and bringing me to know and believe in you. You alone are the Lord, and I will put my trust in none other.

Today's reading: Isaiah 43

SATURDAY

"Forget what happened in the past, and do not dwell on events from long ago. I am going to do something new. It is already happening. Don't you recognize it? I will clear a way in the desert. I will make rivers on dry land." (Isaiah 43:18,19)

Lord, I would like very much for you to do something new in my life. Please make a clear way for me out of this desert and create streams of restoration and rivers of new life to satisfy my dry and thirsty soul.

Today's reading: Psalm 51

SUNDAY

"I will pour water on thirsty ground and rain on dry land. I will pour my Spirit on your offspring and my blessing on your descendants. They will spring up with the grass as poplars spring up by streams." (Isaiah 44:3,4)

Lord, pour out your Spirit on me now. Rain down your kindness and your mercy upon my life. Please don't weary of my cries for your Spirit to rain on me. I will return praises to you as surely as the rain returns to the heavens.

Today's reading: Acts 2

MONDAY

"All these people died having faith. They didn't receive the things that God had promised them, but they saw these things coming in the distant future and rejoiced. They acknowledged that they were living as strangers with no permanent home on earth." (Hebrews 11:13)

I have no permanent home on this earth, as I am only too painfully aware, but I see what is coming and am happy. Much of what you promised in your word I have already tasted, yet much more remains ahead. Lead me on in my journey of faith.

Today's reading: Psalm 144

TUESDAY

"No one can please God without faith. Whoever goes to God must believe that God exists and that he rewards those who seek him." (Hebrews 11:6)

Increase my faith, Lord, for I want to please you with my life. I purpose to seek you with my whole heart and desire that you reward me with your presence. Calm my soul and speak to my troubled heart, and I will run after you.

Today's reading: Hebrews 3

WEDNESDAY

"I am the true vine, and my Father takes care of the vineyard. He removes every one of my branches that doesn't produce fruit. He also prunes every branch that does produce fruit to make it produce more fruit." (John 15:1,2)

There have been seasons of fruitfulness in my life, but I've been in the middle of a long winter, Lord. Life has been cold, desolate and lonely. Please bring the springtime back into my life. Cause your sun to shine again and your moist clouds to drop fresh rain on me. I am your branch. Cause me to be fruitful once again.

Today's reading: Psalm 72

THURSDAY

"Live in me, and I will live in you. A branch cannot produce any fruit by itself. It has to stay attached to the vine. In the same way, you cannot produce fruit unless you live in me. I am the vine. You are the branches. Those who live in me while I live in them will produce a lot of fruit. But you can't produce anything without me." (John 15:4,5)

I see how I have tried in the past, almost unconsciously, to be fruitful apart from you but have had no success. Help me to remain vitally connected with you every day. Early in the morning I will seek you. Throughout the day I will remember you, and at night, on my pillow, I will think of you. In my union with you, I will not strain to produce fruit. I will just watch it happen as a byproduct of being connected to you.

Today's reading: Galatians 5

FRIDAY

"Without prophetic vision people run wild, but blessed are those who follow God's teachings. So live a more disciplined life, and listen carefully to words of knowledge." (Proverbs 29:18, 23:12)

When I catch your vision for this world and recognize my purpose in it, I find discipline naturally flows out of my life. So teach me your word and I will listen carefully.

Today's reading: Psalm 94

SATURDAY

"Do not envy sinners in your heart. Instead, continue to fear the Lord. There is indeed a future, and your hope will never be cut off." (Proverbs 23:17,18)

At times I have envied sinners in my heart. I wonder, how long will they continue to prosper and be at ease when their heart is set against you? I wonder about the future and what you have in store for me, and then I read your word assuring me that, indeed, I do have a future and my hope will never be cut off. I will no longer envy sinners, but pray that through your kindness to them, they may come to repentance.

Today's reading: Psalm 84

SUNDAY

"But he is compassionate. He forgave their sin. He did not destroy them. He restrained his anger many times. He did not display all of his fury. He remembered that they were only flesh and blood, a breeze that blows and does not return." (Psalm 78:38,39)

I am so glad you are a compassionate God who has forgiven my sin. You know that I am weak, made of mere flesh and blood, subject to my frail human condition. Yet, you don't condone sin, but you encourage me to make wise choices and rise above the weakness of my flesh, to walk in the Spirit.

Today's reading: Galatians 5

MONDAY

"Thanks be to the Lord, who daily carries our burdens for us. God is our salvation. Our God is the God of victories. The Almighty Lord is our escape from death." (Psalm 68:19,20)

There are so many benefits in serving you, Lord. I don't know where I'd be if you hadn't been there to carry my burdens during this most difficult trial of my life. You alone grant victory and provide escape from death. Even when I'm laid in the grave, I will escape death and live with you forever. Thanks be to your name.

Today's reading: Psalm 13

TUESDAY

"I want to sing and make music. Wake up, my soul! Wake up, harp and lyre! I want to wake up at dawn. I want to give thanks to you among the people, O Lord." (Psalm 57:7–9)

Wake up my soul, O Lord! Stir me with the greatness of your presence. When I do wake up, praise is not found on my lips, though I wish it were. Lord, I'm still fighting this wet blanket called grief and it's not in a hurry to let go of me. I do want to be among those who joyfully praise you, but for the present it is merely my hope. Please bear with me.

Today's reading: Titus 3

WEDNESDAY

"Keep your tongue from saying evil things and your lips from speaking deceitful things. Turn away from evil, and do good. Seek peace, and pursue it!" (Psalm 34:13,14)

Father, when my spirits are low, my tongue is loose and things are said in haste that should not be spoken. I purpose in my heart to turn away from evil by turning towards that which is good. With all my strength, I will pursue the peace of God, which comes from being in right standing with you. Thank you for your mercy.

Today's reading: Psalm 86

THURSDAY

"Have pity on me, O Lord, because I am in distress. My eyes, my soul, and my body waste away from grief. My life is exhausted from sorrow, my years from groaning." (Psalm 31:9,10)

How long, O Lord, will I continue in this distress? I think I'm doing much better, then suddenly, without warning, the sun withholds its light and dark clouds surround my life. I find myself right back where I was so many months ago. I'm exhausted from sorrow, wasted from grief and in need of your grace.

Today's reading: Psalm 88

FRIDAY

"When this body that decays is changed into a body that cannot decay, and this mortal body is changed into a body that will live forever, then the teaching of Scripture will come true: 'Death is turned into victory! Death, where is your victory? Death, where is your sting?'" (1 Corinthians 15:54,55)

When I wept over the lifeless form of the one I loved so much, lying in the casket just over eight months ago, I never thought I could say, "O death, where is your sting?" At that time, its powerful stinger was fastened securely to my heart, injecting its painful venom, threatening to never let go. I look forward to the day when my body is changed into a body that will never decay, that stinger removed forever. When that happens, Lord, I will rejoice with you that death has turned into victory.

Today's reading: 1 Corinthians 15

SATURDAY

"I put my words in your mouth and sheltered you in the palm of my hand. I stretched out the heavens, laid the foundations of the earth, and said to Zion, 'You are my people.'" (Isaiah 51:16)

Thank you, Lord, for making me part of your family. You have given me wisdom at crucial times and protected me from certain disaster. There is none other like you. Please keep me sheltered in the palm of your hand.

Today's reading: Isaiah 44

SUNDAY

"But now through Christ Jesus you, who were once far away, have been brought near by the blood of Christ." (Ephesians 2:13)

Near, near, I desire to be near you at all times. Though you are with me always, I am rarely aware of your nearness. If I were, I would be spared much heartache and pain. I will draw near to you and you will draw even nearer to me. I will pursue your kingdom and your righteousness and all things I have need of will be added to my life.

Today's reading: Isaiah 48

MONDAY

"This is to continue until all of us are united in our faith and in our knowledge about God's Son, until we become mature, until we measure up to Christ, who is the standard." (Ephesians 4:13)

Lord, you have created me and formed me for your purposes. Through me, you will do great exploits in your perfect timing. As I grow and mature in the knowledge of you, I am being conformed to your image and will continue this process until the day of Jesus Christ. Daily I will draw my strength from you, meeting you in the morning and visiting with you in the evening.

Today's reading: Isaiah 61

TUESDAY

"For this reason, take up all the armor that God supplies. Then you will be able to take a stand during these evil days. Once you have overcome all obstacles, you will be able to stand your ground." (Ephesians 6:13)

Help me to overcome, for the evil day is all around me. It comes in many different forms, some subtle and some obvious. Empower me to see the destructive schemes of the enemy, that I may both expose and destroy them. As I stand firm, please fight for me, and through me, as I boldly use your name. I will draw near you by your blood. In that nearness, give me your strength to defeat all my foes.

Today's reading: Ephesians 6

WEDNESDAY

"It is God who produces in you the desires and actions that please him." (Philippians 2:13)

Father, I know it is your good pleasure to bring me into your will for you desire to prosper me. Not merely in a material sense, but you desire to prosper, develop and release the gifts you have placed in me so that others may come to know you intimately through what they see in me. Thank you for placing your desires in me.

Today's reading: Isaiah 62

THURSDAY

"It's far more than that! I consider everything else worthless because I'm much better off knowing Christ Jesus my Lord. It's because of him that I think of everything as worthless. I threw it all away in order to gain Christ and to have a relationship with him." (Philippians 3:8,9)

I willingly lay down that which I have achieved so that you can accomplish what you desire in the days ahead. I will walk close to you and hear your casual conversation as you speak to my heart the mysteries of your kingdom. Lord, deliver me from my own preoccupations and lead me to walk where you are walking, work where you are working and to rest when you want me to rest.

Today's reading: Psalm 95

FRIDAY

"I will give you treasures from dark places and hidden stockpiles.
Then you will know that I, the Lord God of Israel, have called you
by name." (Isaiah 45:3)

Father, please draw treasure out of the dark and hidden
places of my life where I've known such pain for so long.
Please reveal your glory and your wondrous ways through
the crucible of my life. Use my life, Lord, to proclaim liberty
to other captives and freedom to the oppressed.

Today's reading: Psalm 116

SATURDAY

"O God, you are my God. At dawn I search for you. My soul thirsts
for you. My body longs for you in a dry, parched land where there
is no water." (Psalm 63:1)

I will seek you early, Lord. Before the storm clouds form their
threatening thunderheads, I will seek you, and you will give
me calm in the troubled storm. I will seek you early, often and
continuously, for there is so much I want to learn about you. I
will spend time with you today and learn about you, for you
are meek and lowly of heart, and you will give rest to my soul.

Today's reading: Psalm 66

Week 38

SUNDAY

"Evildoers will be cut off from their inheritance, but those who wait with hope for the Lord will inherit the land." (Psalm 37:9)

I will wait for you, Lord, to strengthen me and uphold me with the power of your goodness. My spirit is willing but my flesh is weak. The sorrow and grief you have brought me through are a pathway to a depth of relationship with you that I've never known before, and I wait, now, with hope, for that to grow.

Today's reading: Psalm 67

MONDAY

"If you love me, you will obey my commandments, and if you obey my commandments, you will live in my love." (John 14:15, 15:10)

I will stay close to you, Lord, as you guide me through this valley of sorrow and grief where death has cast its shadow but can do no more, for you are with me. And when I come through this present difficulty, there is so much more that you have prepared for me, your child, who loves you and keeps your commands.

Today's reading: Acts 5

TUESDAY

"It's me. Don't be afraid! No fear exists where his love is. Rather, perfect love gets rid of fear, because fear involves punishment. The person who lives in fear doesn't have perfect love." (John 6:20, 1 John 4:18)

Father, you have so much to teach me that I cannot understand at this point in my life, but teach me now how to overcome fear. Help me to destroy fear at every turn. When fear comes, I will use your name and begin to thank and praise you until joy springs up in my heart and love and laughter come out of my innermost being. You are the Lord of the wind and the sea, and no circumstance is beyond your control.

Today's reading: Psalm 55

WEDNESDAY

"Jesus said, 'Come!' So Peter got out of the boat and walked on the water toward Jesus. But when he noticed how strong the wind was, he became afraid and started to sink. He shouted, 'Lord, save me!' Immediately, Jesus reached out, caught hold of him and said, 'You have so little faith! Why did you doubt?'" (Matthew 14:29–31)

Sometimes in the past my faith has been more in the power of the wind and the waves than it was in you, who created the wind and sea and established their boundaries and limits. As I stand in the face of this storm, I know with certainty that the God of creation is Lord of even the raging sea. I call upon your name, Jesus. Bring me now to dry land, my destination.

Today's reading: John 6

THURSDAY

"He took Abram outside and said, 'Now look up at the sky and count the stars, if you are able to count them.' He also said to him, 'That's how many descendants you will have!' Then Abram believed the Lord, and the Lord regarded that faith to be his approval of Abram." (Genesis 15:5)

Lord, I believe big things can happen through me after you have completed this work you're doing in me now. It seems big things are accomplished in your kingdom by those who can dream big and have had a big work done in their heart. In faith I will embrace your dreams for me and cast down any vain imaginations that run contrary to your word.

Today's reading: Genesis 12

FRIDAY

"People can't observe the coming of the kingdom of God. They can't say, 'Here it is!' or 'There it is!' You see, the kingdom of God is within you." (Luke 17:20,21)

Lord, I will seek you first in everything and at all times. Show me where you are working in my heart today, for that is where your kingdom is. Remove the weeds and rocks from the soil of my heart and help me to be whole and productive again.

Today's reading: Mark 4

SATURDAY

"Other people are like seeds planted among thorn bushes. They hear the word, but the worries of life, the deceitful pleasures of riches, and the desires for other things take over. They choke the word so that it can't produce anything. Others are like seeds planted on good ground. They hear the word, accept it, and produce crops—thirty, sixty, or one hundred times as much as was planted." (Mark 4:18–20)

Lord, work in my heart like a farmer works in his field. Heal the hard, stony ground of past hurts and show me the misplaced desires that choke out your word. Cause me to be like a piece of reclaimed land that was once stony and covered over with weeds but now has become rich, fertile and fruit-bearing. Father, no field, no matter how neglected or grown over, is beyond your redemptive reach, and with that redemption lies the hope of bountiful harvest.

Today's reading: Matthew 13

Week 39

SUNDAY

"Listen to the word of the Lord, you Israelites. The Lord has brought these charges against those who live in the land: 'There is no faith, no love, and no knowledge of God in the land.'" (Hosea 4:1)

I want to come to know you intimately, Father, through spending time developing my relationship with you. I have become well-acquainted with you in my intellect but not very close in my heart. I have been ever learning but never coming to an intimate knowledge of you. Jesus, you are the truth and desire to live in intimate communion with me in my innermost being. I invite you, earnestly, to do so.

Today's reading: 1 Corinthians 10

MONDAY

"He grew up in his presence like a young tree, like a root out of dry ground. He had no form or majesty that would make us look at him. He had nothing in his appearance that would make us desire him. On that day you will know that I am in my Father and that you are in me and that I am in you." (Isaiah 53:2, John 14:20)

Jesus, when you came to earth in the form of man, you had no special physical traits to cause anyone to notice you. Being fully man, you were also fully God in man. Demons trembled at your presence, diseases fled at your word and every ear turned when you spoke. Now you have chosen to live in me. I am weak and not anything that anyone would notice. But you are strong; your presence, your power, your strength, your love, your joy and your peace dwell in me. Day after day I am being conformed to your image, as I yield to your Spirit living in me.

Today's reading: John 10

TUESDAY

"Come to me, all who are tired from carrying heavy loads, and I will give you rest. I'm leaving you peace. I'm giving you my peace. I don't give you the kind of peace that the world gives. So don't be troubled or cowardly." (Matthew 11:28, John 14:27)

Whenever I begin to lose my sense of peace or whenever that old enemy "fear" comes to encroach, I will come to you. I will breathe your name, and I know you will give me rest. Yes, I will come to you and partake of your love, and fear will flee from me as a cowardly bully flees from a powerful righteous authority.

Today's reading: 2 Timothy 7

WEDNESDAY

"My bones were not hidden from you when I was being made in secret, when I was being skillfully woven in an underground work-shop. I have been so amazingly and miraculously made." (Psalm 139:15,14)

Lord, you have made me unique and special, created for your pleasure to do good works that you have prepared. Please use my unique talents in unique ways to glorify you.

Today's reading: Colossians 2

THURSDAY

"I have written many things for them in my teachings, but they consider these things strange and foreign." (Hosea 8:12)

Admittedly, Lord, I have found many things in your word to be strange and foreign to me. I have viewed your ways, priorities and plans as some strange thing, especially the trials and tribulations of life. But you have said in your word to not think it is strange when the fiery trials test me. Help me to understand that the fiery trials in life are only burning off that which hinders my relationship with you.

Today's reading: Isaiah 1

FRIDAY

"When God tested Abraham, faith led him to offer his son Isaac. Abraham, the one who received the promises from God, was willing to offer his only son as a sacrifice." (Hebrews 11:17)

Father, today I willingly offer on the altar of sacrifice anything that stands between us, hindering the work you have called me to do.

Today's reading: Titus 2

SATURDAY

"Remember, I am with you and will watch over you wherever you go. I will also bring you back to this land because I will not leave you until I do what I've promised you." (Genesis 28:15)

Father, life is a journey where little is certain. You have been with me through all the twists and turns of my journey and have shown me many fearful and wonderful things. I will not fear the rest of the journey, for you are with me and have promised over and over to never leave me.

Today's reading: Nehemiah 9

SUNDAY

"I love those who love me. Those eagerly looking for me will find me. I have riches and honor, lasting wealth and righteousness. What I produce is better than gold, pure gold. What I yield is better than fine silver." (Proverbs 8:17–19)

Father, as I come to read your word in the morning, please enlighten my understanding. The riches I have seen in your word expose gold and silver for the cold, lifeless metals they are. Lord, the treasures in your word are inexhaustible and cannot be compared to earthly riches. Enlarge my heart to contain more of the wealth of your word.

Today's reading: Psalm 119

MONDAY

"Tell those who have the riches of this world not to be arrogant and not to place their confidence in anything as uncertain as riches. Instead, they should place their confidence in God who richly provides us with everything to enjoy." (1 Timothy 6:17)

I'm finding, Lord, as I possess your true riches, that earthly riches are losing their hold on me. To trade the wealth of your word for the uncertain riches of this world would be like trading a son or a daughter for a mere likeness. Many are brought to ruin who pursue temporal riches, but I choose this day to pursue the riches of your kingdom, knowing that you will add whatever temporal things I may need.

Today's reading: Matthew 6

TUESDAY

"Also, at that time you were without Christ. You were excluded from citizenship in Israel, and the pledges God made in his promise were foreign to you. You had no hope and were in the world without God." (Ephesians 2:12)

I well remember the time that I had no part in your promises, Lord. But you loved me unconditionally when I was still dead in my sins and without hope in this world. Now my heart is turned towards you and you have made me accepted in the Beloved. Because of this, I will approach you boldly, confidently and without fear of reproach.

Today's reading: Psalm 115

WEDNESDAY

"Don't love the world and what it offers. Those who love the world don't have the Father's love in them. Not everything that the world offers—physical gratification, greed, and extravagant lifestyles— comes from the Father. It comes from the world, and the world

and its evil desires are passing away. But the person who does what God wants lives forever." (1 John 2:15–17)

I set my affections on you today and humble myself under your mighty hand. I submit myself to your word and its authority, resisting the devil and the temptations he brings. I will be steadfast in the faith and will watch as you crush Satan under my feet.

Today's reading: Psalm 122

THURSDAY

"There isn't any temptation that you have experienced which is unusual for humans. God, who faithfully keeps his promises, will not allow you to be tempted beyond your power to resist. But when you are tempted, he will also give you the ability to endure the temptation as your way of escape." (1 Corinthians 10:13)

Lord, the temptations of this life pull on me, but they aren't anything uncommon, and you, the God of grace, always provide a way of escape. These trials and temptations of life test my faith and reveal its trustworthiness. In the end, patience is produced, which leads to maturity, completeness and sufficiency in all things.

Today's reading: Psalm 132

FRIDAY

"I have been crucified with Christ. I no longer live, but Christ lives in me. The life I now live I live by believing in God's Son, who loved me and took the punishment for my sins." (Galatians 2:19,20)

I believe in the Son of God, who was born of a virgin, lived a sinless life, was crucified for me and arose from the dead that I might live with him forevermore. Thank you for this priceless gift.

Today's reading: Psalm 149

SATURDAY

"Dear friends, since you are foreigners and temporary residents in the world, I'm encouraging you to keep away from the desires of your corrupt nature. These desires constantly attack you." (1 Peter 2:11)

These desires of my corrupt nature seem to wage war in my soul. My emotions, intellect and will are all tested when that corrupt nature rears its ugly head. I ask you, Father, to renew my intellect, free my emotions and be the Lord of my will.

Today's reading: Proverbs 11

Week 41

SUNDAY

"Live your life as your spiritual nature directs you. Then you will never follow through on what your corrupt nature wants."
(Galatians 5:16)

My spiritual nature directs me to spend more time with you, Lord. I find that when I let the preoccupations of life distract me from some quiet time with you, temptation increases in both strength and frequency. At times like these I will draw near to you, and you have promised to draw near to me. In your name I will resist the wicked one, and he will flee from me.

Today's reading: Galatians 5

MONDAY

"Always be joyful. Never stop praying. Whatever happens, give thanks. Hold on to what is good. Keep away from every kind of evil." (1 Thessalonians 5:16–18,21,22)

Out of prayer comes joy. Out of joy comes thanks, and I have so much to be thankful for, even in the face of what I have lost. Today I give you thanks, holding on to every good thing from the past, every fond memory and dream, knowing that all that I have in life, every good and perfect gift, comes from you, Father.

Today's reading: Psalm 114

TUESDAY

*"Jesus told them, 'I have food to eat that you don't know about....
My food is to do what the one who sent me wants me to do and to
finish the work he has given me.'"* (John 4:32,34)

Lord, all my life you have been molding me and arranging
circumstances to conform to your will for my life. You have
placed a sense of destiny within me, but instead of trying to
pursue that destiny or calling, I will pursue you. I ask you to
bring me into my destiny in your time.

Today's reading: John 6

WEDNESDAY

*"Whoever doesn't take up his cross and follow me doesn't deserve
to be my disciple. The person who tries to preserve his life will lose
it, but the person who loses his life for me will preserve it."*
(Matthew 10:38,39)

I will take up my cross today and follow you, Lord. I will
pursue you, for you are my destiny. In following you, I will
reach new heights and from that new vantage point begin to
comprehend your true purposes for my life.

Today's reading: Proverbs 15

THURSDAY

"Then the Lord answered me, 'Write the vision. Make it clear on tablets so that anyone can read it quickly. The vision will still happen at the appointed time. It hurries toward its goal. It won't be a lie. If it's delayed, wait for it. It will certainly happen. It won't be late.'" (Habakkuk 2:2,3)

Lord, write your vision for me on the tablet of my heart. In the meantime, I will first seek your kingdom and seek to walk in right relationship with you. The plans you have for my life will be revealed in me, not discovered, and that revealing process will come from having communion with you.

Today's reading: Psalm 33

FRIDAY

"However, if my people, who are called by my name, will humble themselves, pray, search for me, and turn from their evil ways, then I will hear their prayer from heaven, forgive their sins, and heal their country." (2 Chronicles 7:14)

Father, as I humble myself, pray, search for you and turn away from that which is evil, show yourself strong in my life. Heal not only the country or land I live in, but heal that land within my heart, which still produces thorns in desolate places. As I pursue you, please heal my heart so good may flow out of it.

Today's reading: Mark 2

SATURDAY

"Pursue them with your storms, and terrify them with your wind-storms the way fire burns a forest and flames set mountains on fire. Let their faces blush with shame, O Lord, so that they must look to you for help." (Psalm 83:14–16)

I hate to admit it, Lord, but had it not been for many of the terrifying storms in my life, I wouldn't have pressed into my relationship with you. But even in that, you always rescue me and deliver me from the hot furnace of affliction, never relenting in your love for me.

Today's reading: Exodus 3

Week 42

SUNDAY

"It is good to give thanks to the Lord, because he is good, because his mercy endures forever, and because it is God's will in Christ Jesus that you do this." (Psalm 92:1, 1 Chronicles 16:34, 1 Thessalonians 5:18)

O Lord, when my heart is thankful, all that you've spoken to me seems to put down roots and flourish. But when I'm ungrateful and critical, those hopes and dreams evade me, withering in the heat of affliction. Therefore, I cultivate an attitude of gratitude and watch as even my trust in you increases.

Today's reading: Romans 1

MONDAY

"Keep your tongue from saying evil things and your lips from speaking deceitful things, for even before there is a single word on your tongue, the Lord knows all about it. Everyone should be quick to listen, slow to speak, and should not get angry easily. An angry person doesn't do what God approves of." (Psalm 34:13, 139:4, James 1:19,20)

As I watch my reactions to people throughout the day, I find myself saying things I regret. I choose today to view those who wrong me as garden tools simply exposing a hard, stony area in my heart. When that happens, Lord, I will choose to forgive and ask you to heal that stony area in my heart.

Today's reading: Psalm 73

~

TUESDAY

"We can't allow ourselves to get tired of living the right way. Certainly, each of us will receive everlasting life at the proper time, if we don't give up. In the meantime, God's divine power has given us every-thing we need for life and for godliness. This power was given to us through knowledge of the one who called us by his own glory and integrity." (Galatians 6:9, 2 Peter 1:3)

When I need a friend, Lord, you are a friend that stays closer than a brother. When I need a Father, you call me your child. When I need a strong warrior to defend me, you are that as well. You are all that I need now and ever will need.

Today's reading: Deuteronomy 8

~

WEDNESDAY

"Do your best to present yourself to God as a tried-and-true worker who isn't ashamed to teach the word of truth correctly." (2 Timothy 2:15)

For me to be able to teach your word to anyone, I must first study and understand the message it contains. Help me to become skillful in the daily application of your word, Lord. Open my eyes, that I may see the glory of the mystery of the gospel of Jesus Christ. Help me to interpret my grief through your word instead of interpreting your word through my grief.

Today's reading: 2 Timothy 2

THURSDAY

"God's promise that we may enter his place of rest still stands. Yes, a time of rest and worship exists for God's people. Those who entered his place of rest also rested from their work as God did from his. So we must make every effort to enter that place of rest."
(Hebrews 4:1,9–11)

Rest seems to be more a state of mind than an absence of labor. By allowing you to be at the center of my thoughts, by bringing you all my prayers of anguish on the wings of thanksgiving, I find perfect peace and rest. Help me to rest in you as I do the work you have called me to do.

Today's reading: Deuteronomy 12

FRIDAY

"Be happy with the Lord, and he will give you the desires of your heart. Entrust your ways to the Lord. Trust him, and he will act on your behalf." (Psalm 37:4,5)

My happiness is indeed found in you, Lord. I entrust my ways to you and purpose to never let the work I do be done through lack of trust, for that is wrong and leads to futility. The work I do, as I recover from this grief and move forward in life, will be spurred on by trust and confident expectation, accomplishing much.

Today's reading: Jeremiah 17

SATURDAY

"Turn all your anxiety over to God because he cares for you." (1 Peter 5:7)

Show me, Lord, when I fail to bring my cares to you to let you work them out for my good. When I lose that sense of peace, remind me to turn all my anxiety over to you because you care for me. In doing so, I will find quietness and rest. Help me to learn that you and you alone offer tranquillity and freedom from hopelessness.

Today's reading: Psalm 79

Week 43

SUNDAY

"A trustworthy person has many blessings, but anyone in a hurry to get rich will not escape punishment." (Proverbs 28:20)

Father, so often I find myself in a hurry about life in general. Somehow the pace of life has picked up, and in trying to make ends meet, I've been extremely busy. Help me to slow down and remember who you created me to be.

Today's reading: Romans 3

MONDAY

"You are partners with Christ Jesus because of God. Jesus has become our wisdom sent from God, our righteousness, our holiness, and our ransom from sin." (1 Corinthians 1:30)

What I do should flow out of who I am, instead of who I am being determined by what I do. I need to be reminded that I am your child and a partner with Jesus Christ, and that you, Lord, want to produce in me the desires and actions that please you. With that in mind, what I do in the days ahead will be determined by who I really am. As this reality sinks into my subconscious thinking, even the world around me will perceive me differently.

Today's reading: Romans 4

TUESDAY

"From the creation of the world, God's invisible qualities, his eternal power and divine nature, have been clearly observed in what he made." (Romans 1:20)

It seems, Lord, that what I can see and touch of your created order is a physical manifestation of your spiritual character. Similarly, when others see me, they see a reflection of who I am spiritually. Help me to become strong in you, conformed to the image and character of your Spirit.

Today's reading: Romans 9

WEDNESDAY

"The greatest love you can show is to give your life for your friends. You are my friends if you obey my commandments. Christ died for us while we were still sinners. This demonstrates God's love for us." (John 15:13, Romans 5:8)

Father, I can't earn your love or merit your forgiveness, but neither can I outrun it. I can only reject it. Many times I slip and stumble along life's way and quickly condemn myself, only to find that you were waiting for me with outstretched arms. How quick I've been to condemn myself and judge myself unworthy to receive your kindness. But you, Lord, have made me worthy by the blood of Jesus

Christ, and I can now freely approach your throne of grace in my time of need.

Today's reading: Romans 10

THURSDAY

"In the morning, O Lord, hear my voice. In the morning I lay my needs in front of you, and I wait." (Psalm 5:3)

So often, Lord, the cares of life rob me of life itself by severing my communion with you. It is that communion that gives me the life-flow to handle the day. It is in that communion time that I receive your life, like the branch receives its life from the vine. You are the vine, Lord. Let your life flow into me, that I may be fruitful and increase.

Today's reading: Romans 11

FRIDAY

"Christ has freed us so that we may enjoy the benefits of freedom. Therefore, be firm in this freedom, and don't become slaves again." (Galatians 5:1)

There is such freedom in your kingdom, Lord—and I am in your kingdom and your kingdom is in me. I am yours and you live in me. Help me to not become a slave again to my own selfish desires or anything else that would hinder my relationship with you. Free me from any work or deed done in my own strength that I use to supply my needs apart from you.

Today's reading: Romans 13

SATURDAY

"Blessed is the nation whose God is the Lord. Blessed are the people he has chosen as his own." (Psalm 33:12)

Father, you have chosen me as your own, to be your great treasure. I have become your inheritance, and you have become mine. Words cannot express my gratitude. Understandably, I am thrilled to be able to call the king of the universe my Father, but what really amazes me is that you are thrilled to call me your child!

Today's reading: Acts 10

SUNDAY

"So change the way you think and act, and turn to God to have your sins removed. Then times will come when the Lord will refresh you. He will send you Jesus, whom he has appointed to be the Christ." (Acts 3:19,20)

Make this a day when you come and refresh me, Lord. I come to you now to tap into that cool, refreshing spring of living water that you promised the woman at the well. I'm dry and thirsty and need to drink of your living wells that never run dry.

Today's reading: Isaiah 44

MONDAY

"When he went back to the disciples, he found them asleep. He said to Peter, 'Couldn't you stay awake with me for one hour? Stay awake, and pray that you won't be tempted. You want to do what's right, but you're weak.'" (Matthew 26:40,41)

I need to gain a sense of your presence, your peace and your joy, Lord, before I go out into the hustle and bustle of this world. I will be alert and watchful for your instructions, looking for you to guide my every step.

Today's reading: Luke 22

TUESDAY

"The tongue has the power of life and death, and those who love to talk will have to eat their own words. May the words from my mouth and the thoughts from my heart be acceptable to you, O LORD, my rock and my defender." (Proverbs 18:21, Psalm 19:14)

Father, help me to say more with fewer words. Too often I speak without having first measured my words, considered their impact, or removed my self-interest from them. Fill my mouth with your words that I may gladden the heart of the hearer.

Today's reading: Proverbs 15

WEDNESDAY

"You are not happy with any sacrifice. Otherwise, I would offer one to you. You are not pleased with burnt offerings. The sacrifice pleasing to God is a broken spirit. O God, you do not despise a broken and sorrowful heart." (Psalm 51:16,17)

Lord, you desire brokenness in the inward parts, but you will not leave us broken. Nearly ten months ago, I was more than broken, I was shattered like a vase dropped from a twelve story rooftop. The world as I knew it came to an abrupt end with no apparent hope in sight. Then you came, first to comfort me, then to slowly put the pieces of my life together.

There is much to do in that regard, but one day you will have reconstructed my life, the same, yet so different from the one that fell from the rooftop.

Today's reading: Isaiah 42

THURSDAY

"Praise the LORD, my soul, and never forget all the good he has done: He is the one who forgives all your sins, the one who heals all your diseases, the one who rescues your life from the pit, the one who crowns you with mercy and compassion, the one who fills your life with blessings so that you become young again like an eagle." (Psalm 103:2–5)

How could I ever forget all the good you have done, Lord? You have forgiven and healed me. When my life was in a pit, you rescued me and covered me with mercy and compassion. Knowing what you have done for me in the past gives me hope for a brighter future.

Today's reading: Colossians 1

FRIDAY

"He certainly knows what we are made of. He bears in mind that we are dust. Human life is as short-lived as grass. It blossoms like a

flower in the field. When the wind blows over the flower, it disap-
pears, and there is no longer any sign of it." (Psalm 103:14–16)

Life is short, then you die. Soon, no one remembers you.
Those who do remember die also. It all seems so futile, Father,
if it weren't for the fact that we have an opportunity here on
earth to accept and acknowledge your Son, Jesus Christ, in
front of others, so we can be accepted and acknowledged by
Jesus in front of you. In this way, we can spend eternity with
you, where we will never be forgotten.

Today's reading: Matthew 10

SATURDAY

"I will find joy in the LORD. I will delight in my God. He has
dressed me in the clothes of salvation. He has wrapped me in the
robe of righteousness like a bridegroom with a priest's turban, like
a bride with her jewels." (Isaiah 61:10)

When joy seems to evade me, I will find you, and in finding
you, Lord, I will find joy. I will think about what you have
saved me from and how you clothed me with a robe of righteousness so that I could be in right standing with you. I will
think on these things and be glad.

Today's reading: Isaiah 61

SUNDAY

"We know that if the life we live here on earth is ever taken down like a tent, we still have a building from God. It is an eternal house in heaven that isn't made by human hands. While we are in this tent, we sigh. We feel distressed because we don't want to take off the tent, but we do want to put on the eternal house. Then eternal life will put an end to our mortal existence." (2 Corinthians 5:1,4)

Many have gone to be with you, Lord, and now that I have a loved one who has joined you so recently, I am all the more interested in heaven. Thank you for giving me glimpses through your word of what life is like for my loved one.

Today's reading: Psalm 8

MONDAY

"Stop forming inappropriate relationships with unbelievers. Can right and wrong be partners? Can light have anything in common with darkness? Can God's temple contain false gods? Clearly, we are the temple of the living God." (2 Corinthians 6:14,16)

Lord, help me to discern appropriate relationships with others. As I form new friendships and explore new opportunities, I want to carefully choose those with whom I closely associate. I still feel very vulnerable since my loss and am concerned that I may make poor choices in moments of weakness. Please help me with this.

Today's reading: 1 Corinthians 3

TUESDAY

"While they were being severely tested by suffering, their overflowing joy, along with their extreme poverty, has made them even more generous." (2 Corinthians 8:2)

Lord, teach me the secret to overflowing joy during a time of severe testing. Let me see what these saints of old who were persecuted unto death saw. Bring me to the level of relationship they had with you that made this possible. Give me a spirit of generosity that actually increases during times of extreme poverty.

Today's reading: Philippians 4

WEDNESDAY

"God gives seed to the farmer and food to those who need to eat. God will also give you seed and multiply it. In your lives he will increase the things you do that have his approval. God will make you rich enough so that you can always be generous." (2 Corinthians 9:10,11)

Seeds, yes seeds! You have given me many seeds in the form of dreams, visions and ideas. They were planted in the soil of my heart. Many times the worries or cares I carried choked out the dreams and therefore my dreams did not produce fruit. Other times, when others questioned my dreams, I abandoned them because of the wounded places in my heart. Yes, you have given me all that I need in the form of seeds. I will water them, nurture them and wait for them, and they will surely produce a harvest.

Today's reading: Mark 4

THURSDAY

"You were indeed called to be free, brothers and sisters. Don't turn this freedom into an excuse for your corrupt nature to express itself. Rather, serve each other through love." (Galatians 5:13)

Father, indeed you have called us into great freedom and liberty. Give me opportunity to use this freedom to serve my fellow human in love. I used to think freedom was the ability to do whatever I wanted, whenever I wanted. I now realize that freedom is the ability to do the right thing at any given time. When I use freedom to satisfy my own corrupt nature, I'm really back in bondage again. Today, I will express my freedom by serving your purposes in love.

Today's reading: 1 Corinthians 8

FRIDAY

"Praise the God and Father of our Lord Jesus Christ! Through Christ, God has blessed us with every spiritual blessing that heaven has to offer." (Ephesians 1:3)

Truly every spiritual blessing is mine through union with your Son, Jesus Christ. Being grafted onto the vine and staying united with him will cause all that I need for life and godliness to flow quite naturally into my life. I will not need to strive for these things.

Today's reading: John 15

SATURDAY

"Before the creation of the world, he chose us through Christ to be holy and perfect in his presence." (Ephesians 1:4)

Before you ever created the world, I was on your mind. You chose me to be holy and perfect, even as you are holy and perfect. You made this possible through Christ's death on the cross. Because of your great love, you made a decision to adopt me into your family. You alone, O Lord, are worthy to be praised!

Today's reading: Jeremiah 1

Week 46

SUNDAY

*"I pray that the glorious Father, the God of our Lord Jesus Christ,
would give you a spirit of wisdom and revelation as you come to
know Christ better. Then you will have deeper insight. You will
know the confidence that he calls you to have and the glorious
wealth that God's people will inherit. You will also know the
unlimited greatness of his power as it works with might and
strength for us, the believers."* (Ephesians 1:17 -19)

Wisdom and revelation are truly spiritual gifts that come from
you, Father, as we come to know you better. They seem to be
more "caught" than "taught," serving as tools to give us deeper insight into the hope of your calling, the wealth of God-
given potential within us, and the great power working on
our behalf behind the scenes.

Today's reading: Ephesians 1

MONDAY

*"Glory belongs to God, whose power is at work in us. By this
power he can do infinitely more than we can ask or imagine."*
(Ephesians 3:20)

Lord, I know your power is at work in me, but all too often I feel like I'm plugged into a burned out flashlight battery, rather than into the power that created the universe. I know your power hasn't diminished, so I want to clean off the corroded terminals of my heart and get firmly plugged in to your power. Let the same power that raised Christ from the dead surge through my spirit and accomplish through me far more than I have ever asked or thought.

Today's reading: Hebrews 12

TUESDAY

"I, a prisoner in the Lord, encourage you to live the kind of life which proves that God has called you. Be humble and gentle in every way. Be patient with each other and lovingly accept each other. Through the peace that ties you together, do your best to maintain the unity that the Spirit gives." (Ephesians 4:1–3)

You have made me a new creature in Christ. Now I must learn to live like one. Just like a baby learns to walk, I'm going to have to learn to walk all over again as this new creature, and in so doing, go on to maturity in Christ.

Today's reading: Ephesians 4

WEDNESDAY

"Be angry without sinning. Don't go to bed angry. Don't give the devil any opportunity to work." (Ephesians 4:26)

Teach me to resolve conflict, Lord. Show me how to be angry without sinning or giving the devil any opportunity to work. Help me to resolve unresolved anger over the unalterable losses of the past.

Today's reading: Matthew 18

THURSDAY

"So then, be very careful how you live. Don't live like foolish people but like wise people. Make the most of your opportunities because these are evil days." (Ephesians 5:16,17)

Wise people discern providential opportunities and seize them, while foolish people talk about opportunities and miss them. Teach me, Lord, to discern those fleeting moments of time when a special opportunity presents itself, and give me the courage to seize it.

Today's reading: Proverbs 3

FRIDAY

"Sing and make music to the Lord with your hearts. Always thank God the Father for everything in the name of our Lord Jesus Christ." (Ephesians 5:19,20)

Lord, help me to tune in to the music of heaven. Put a melody in my heart that plays throughout the day. Give me a psalm, a hymn or a spiritual song that unites my heart with your higher purposes and draws me into an awareness of your abiding presence.

Today's reading: Psalm 148

SATURDAY

"Imitate God, since you are the children he loves. Live in love as Christ also loved us. He gave his life for us as an offering and sacrifice, a soothing aroma to God." (Ephesians 5:1,2)

Love was your idea, Father, and you initiated it. We love you because you first loved us. Now, I choose to initiate love instead of waiting for others to initiate it with me. I am no longer going to wait to receive love before I give it. I'm going to imitate you and initiate love, and you, who see in secret, will reward openly.

Today's reading: 1 John 3

Week 47

SUNDAY

"Put on all the armor that God supplies. In this way you can take a stand against the devil's strategies. This is not a wrestling match against a human opponent. We are wrestling with rulers, authorities, the powers who govern this world of darkness, and spiritual forces that control evil in the heavenly world." (Ephesians 6:11,12)

I recognize that my fight is not with other people but with a master schemer who governs the world of darkness. I can't fight him on his terms and with his weapons and win. So I will take the weapons and armor that you offer, Lord, and stand firm in your name and authority and watch you give me the victory.

Today's reading: Ephesians 6

MONDAY

"Pray in the Spirit in every situation. Use every kind of prayer and request there is. For the same reason be alert. Use every kind of effort and make every kind of request for all of God's people." (Ephesians 6:18)

Life is like a mine field, and I need the leading of the Holy Spirit on a daily basis to avoid the many hidden land mines the enemy has laid for me. I will pray always, in every situation, using all the gifts and discernment you, Father, have given me. I will extend my prayers beyond my own household and ask you to have others praying for me.

Today's reading: 1 Thessalonians 5

TUESDAY

"I'm convinced that God, who began this good work in you, will carry it through to completion on the day of Christ Jesus."
(Philippians 1:6)

Lord, almost a year ago I was hanging by a thread in this world, not at all sure that any good work was ever going to be completed in me. Now, all these months later, I can see healing taking place and a sense of purpose coming back into my life like never before. I am now convinced that you, who started this good work, will carry it through to completion in me.

Today's reading: Philippians 1

WEDNESDAY

"I eagerly expect and hope that I will have nothing to be ashamed of. I will speak very boldly and honor Christ in my body, now as always, whether I live or die. Christ means everything to me in this life, and when I die I'll have even more." (Philippians 1:20,21)

As long as I live on this earth, I will honor you in my body, Lord. You mean everything to me, and as long as I have breath, I will praise you. As long as I have strength, I will serve you. Here I stand, I can do no less. God, help me.

Today's reading: Psalm 111

THURSDAY

"So don't let your opponents intimidate you in any way. This is God's way of showing them that they will be destroyed and that you will be saved." (Philippians 1:28)

I will no longer allow terror or fear to grip my heart. I will allow the personality of Christ to take control of my life. Then my opponents will back down. In fact, Father, you have promised that no weapon formed against me will prosper, and every tongue that rises up against me in judgment I have the right to condemn. I will walk in the confidence you have for me today.

Today's reading: Psalm 139

FRIDAY

"Have the same attitude that Christ Jesus had. Although he was in the form of God and equal with God, he did not take advantage of his equality. Instead, he emptied himself by taking on the form of a servant, by becoming like other humans, by having a human appearance. He humbled himself by becoming obedient to the point of death, death on a cross." (Philippians 2:5–8)

Father, I choose today to embrace the attitudes that Jesus exemplified. Though I am a child of the king of kings, I will lead through serving others, not thinking more highly of myself than I ought. I will walk in humility, remembering from where you have brought me, and I will obey right away, even if it hurts.

Today's reading: Proverbs 22

SATURDAY

"He created all things in heaven and on earth, visible and invisible. Whether they are kings or lords, rulers or powers—everything has been created through him and for him." (Colossians 1:16)

Father, you created me for your good pleasure. In fact, nothing exists that you didn't create. I will think on that and reverence your name.

Today's reading: Job 38

Week 48

SUNDAY

"In the past God hid this mystery, but now he has revealed it to his people. God wanted his people throughout the world to know the glorious riches of this mystery—which is Christ living in you, giving you the hope of glory" (Colossians 1:26,27)

Let the power and love of Christ live in me, surge through me and be released out of me to a sick and dying world. I will share this hope of glory, Christ in me, with the world around me and invite others to share in the glorious riches which come from this joyous union.

Today's reading: Philippians 2

MONDAY

"Since you were brought back to life with Christ, focus on the things that are above—where Christ holds the highest position. Keep your mind on things above, not on worldly things. You have died, and your life is hidden with Christ in God." (Colossians 3:1–3)

Show me ways, Lord, to store up treasures in heaven, for you taught us that where our treasure is, there would be our heart also. Today, I set my affection on things above and look for ways to pursue your priorities and advance your kingdom.

Today's reading: Deuteronomy 30

TUESDAY

"God made a promise to Abraham. Since he had no one greater on whom to base his oath, he based it on himself. He said, 'I will certainly bless you and give you many descendants.' So Abraham received what God promised because he waited patiently for it." (Hebrews 6:13–15)

I will wait patiently for you, Lord, knowing that every good and perfect gift that I need in this life will come from you in your timing. Instead of being in a hurry, I will only go where you lead, when you lead. Though this does not mean that everything will go smoothly, I know that no opposition will come that you don't allow and that I can't handle in your name.

Today's reading: Malachi 3

WEDNESDAY

"But this is the promise that I will make to Israel after those days, says the Lord: I will put my teachings inside them, and I will write those teachings on their hearts. I will be their God and they will be my people." (Hebrews 8:10)

Your laws, O Lord, are written on my heart, and I long to keep them because you are my God. I will retreat into your presence and commune with you in my heart, to learn of you and to know intimately your ways. Instruct my heart, O Lord.

Today's reading: Psalm 16

THURSDAY

"Likewise, Christ was sacrificed once to take away the sins of humanity, and after that he will appear a second time. This time he will not deal with sin, but he will save those who eagerly wait for him." (Hebrews 9:28)

Jesus, you came from heaven to earth to show me the way, and to pay my debt. I eagerly await your imminent return, but until that day, I will occupy myself in your kingdom, finding opportune ways to increase your kingdom and to enhance your reputation.

Today's reading: Galatians 2

FRIDAY

"My brothers and sisters, be very happy when you are tested in different ways. You know that such testing of your faith produces endurance. Endure until your testing is over. Then you will be mature and complete, and you won't need anything." (James 1:2–4)

Lord, the tests of life burn like fire. Help me to endure the heat of this test like a piece of silver being melted in a melting pot must endure the heat of the silversmith. Don't remove me from the test until the dross is removed, otherwise I will just have to go through this flame again. Complete the work you have begun in me. Turn up the flame and melt me.

Remove the dross and pour me into the unique form you created me to be, that I may serve you with honor.

Today's reading: Romans 9

SATURDAY

"Do what God's word says. Don't merely listen to it, or you will fool yourselves. If someone listens to God's word but doesn't do what it says, he is like a person who looks at his face in a mirror, studies his features, goes away, and immediately forgets what he looks like. However, the person who continues to study God's perfect teachings that make people free and who remains committed to them will be blessed. People like that don't merely listen and forget; they actually do what God's teachings say." (James 1:22–25)

Lord, it seems that life is a training field with your word as the instruction manual. Lead me through life experiences where I can practice what I have learned in your presence. Show me through the trials of life what is built on sand and what will stand the test of time.

Today's reading: Psalm 31

Week 49

SUNDAY

"I love the LORD because he hears my voice, my pleas for mercy. I will call on him as long as I live because he turns his ear toward me." (Psalm 116:1,2)

Lord, right now, I call out to you for your tender mercy, knowing that your ear is always cocked in my direction. I will call and you will answer because you always hear my cry for help and answer me. Your heart is always ready to respond to my pleas for mercy. When you answer, I will linger in your presence and be restored.

Today's reading: Jeremiah 33

MONDAY

"You make the path of life known to me. Complete joy is in your presence. Pleasures are by your side forever." (Psalm 16:11)

Father, flood my soul with a conscious awareness of your presence today. For in your presence I truly find the fountain of eternal life. The mysteries of the universe are found in your presence. When I am weary, I will come into your presence and find rest. When I am grieving a loss, I will come into your presence and find comfort. When I just need to smile again, I will come into your presence and find joy.

Today's reading: Psalm 16

TUESDAY

"We have been born into a new life which has an inheritance that can't be destroyed or corrupted and can't fade away. That inheritance is kept in heaven for you, since you are guarded by God's power through faith for a salvation that is ready to be revealed at the end of time." (1 Peter 1:4,5)

Father, what you have reserved for me in heaven cannot be stolen, neither can it be lost. Indeed, you have reserved such a great treasure for me that no earthly counterpart can compare. Not only is this inheritance reserved safely beyond the reach of corruption, but you have sent your power to guard me through faith until that great and wonderful day when I see the treasure in heaven.

Today's reading: Psalm 135

WEDNESDAY

"You are extremely happy about these things, even though you have to suffer different kinds of trouble for a little while now. The purpose of these troubles is to test your faith as fire tests how genuine gold is. Your faith is more precious than gold, and by passing the test, it gives praise, glory, and honor to God. This will happen when Jesus Christ appears again." (1 Peter 1:6,7)

I am beginning to see the importance of different kinds of troubles, Lord. Your word says that it is impossible to please you without faith, and that we are guarded by your power through faith. These trials test our faith, enabling us to see the condition of our faith. Many times I have thought I was strong in the faith until the storm came, and I found out how weak my faith really was. Thank you for the tests that allow me to see what you already know, so that I can build up my faith and do that which is pleasing to you.

Today's reading: Malachi 3

THURSDAY

"Love each other with a warm love that comes from the heart. After all, you have purified yourselves by obeying the truth. As a result you have a sincere love for each other." (1 Peter 1:22)

Father, there are so many others who are in need of comfort and love who are just now beginning the journey of grief that I began so many months ago. Yes, my heart is very tender and tears are never far from the surface, but I know the pain that others are going through, and I am willing to reach out to them with a warmth of love that you have given me.

Today's reading: 2 Corinthians 1

FRIDAY

"However, you are chosen people, a royal priesthood, a holy nation, people who belong to God. You were chosen to tell about

the excellent qualities of God, who called you out of darkness into his marvelous light." (1 Peter 2:9)

Father, you have pulled me out of such a dark pit and brought me into your marvelous light. I want to tell everyone about your excellent qualities: how much you love me, how patient you are, how kind, gracious and generous you are. And best of all, I can share all these things out of my own personal experience!

Today's reading: Psalm 117

SATURDAY

"Christ never committed any sin. He never spoke deceitfully. Christ never verbally abused those who verbally abused him. When he suffered, he didn't make any threats but left everything to the one who judges fairly." (1 Peter 2:22,23)

Father, there are many who have judged me when it wasn't their place to do so. Others have caused personal pain with their unkind words. Forgive me for my unkind response at times. Now I choose to purposefully leave those people in your hands as the only one who knows the conditions of all our hearts and can judge fairly. One thing I have learned: "Hurting people hurt others. Healed people heal others."

Today's reading: 1 Samuel 16

Week 50

SUNDAY

"God's divine power has given us everything we need for life and for godliness. This power was given to us through knowledge of the one who called us by his own glory and integrity." (2 Peter 1:3)

Father, when I try to be godly, I soon burn out and fail, but when I just spend time with you, I become more like you and thus acquire godliness. Thank you for your divine power which is at work in me, energized by love and released by faith to give me everything I need in this life.

Today's reading: John 15

MONDAY

"Because of this, make every effort to add integrity to your faith; and to integrity add knowledge; to knowledge add self-control; to self-control add endurance; to endurance add godliness; to godliness add Christian affection; and to Christian affection add love. If you have these qualities and they are increasing, it demonstrates that your knowledge about our Lord Jesus Christ is living and productive." (2 Peter 1:5–8)

These wonderful Christian virtues are a by-product of an intimate relationship with you, Lord. Help me to know you and to comprehend the scope of your love. Let me sit under the spout of your knowledge and tap into the flow of your wisdom. Lead me through the trials of life to produce faith, endurance and self-control. Perfect godliness in me as you reveal your character through your word, your creation and your Holy Spirit.

Today's reading: 2 Peter 1

TUESDAY

"Since the Lord did all this, he knows how to rescue godly people when they are tested." (2 Peter 2:9)

Father, you didn't promise that I would escape the fire, only that I wouldn't be burned. You didn't promise that floods wouldn't come, only that I wouldn't drown. You didn't say there wouldn't be storms, only that I could pass through them. Surely, you know how to rescue godly people when they are in trouble.

Today's reading: 2 Peter 2

WEDNESDAY

"Whenever our conscience condemns us, we will be reassured that God is greater than our conscience and knows everything. Dear friends, if our conscience doesn't condemn us, we can boldly look to God and receive from him anything we ask." (1 John 3:20,21)

According to your word, Lord, my conscience has been cleansed by the blood of Jesus Christ. Yet all too often I have held back from asking anything of you because of my own sense of guilt. Thank you for reminding me that you are greater than my conscience, and I am always welcome in your presence.

Today's reading: 1 John 3

THURSDAY

"Those who obey Christ's commandments live in God, and God lives in them. We know that he lives in us because he has given us the Spirit." (1 John 3:24)

You live in those who keep your commandments. You live in them and give them life. Your life in me produces fruit in the form of new values, changed character, restored relationships, a healed heart, occasional outbursts of sheer joy and your love spread about my heart by the Holy Spirit.

Today's reading: Romans 5

FRIDAY

"Dear friends, we must love each other because love comes from God. Everyone who loves has been born from God and knows

God. The person who doesn't love doesn't know God, because God is love." (1 John 4:7,8)

The one abiding quality, the unmistakable signature of the Lord Jesus Christ is pure, unmerited love. Lord, I have freely received your love and will freely share it with others. The world is love-starved, yet your love is limitless and deposited in the heart of every believer. Love, like faith, requires action, even risk. Today I will step out in faith and love my neighbor, and I will watch how you touch his or her life through me.

Today's reading: 1 Peter 4

SATURDAY

"With a lot of wisdom comes a lot of heartache. The greater your knowledge, the greater your pain." (Ecclesiastes 1:18)

Lord, in my innocence, I asked for much wisdom and received much heartache. In the naiveté of my youth, I asked for great knowledge and received great pain, and in the process of it all, I find they are inseparable. Now as I stand haltingly at the door of commitment, I ponder the price of great love, and all I can see is you hanging on a tree. What love! What price! God, help me!

Today's reading: John 15

Week 51

SUNDAY

"I call aloud to the LORD, and he answers me from his holy mountain. I lie down and sleep. I wake up again because the LORD continues to support me. I am not afraid of tens of thousands who have taken positions against me on all sides." (Psalm 3:4–6)

Lord, despite the obstacles in front of me and the tormentors behind me, I will find both peace in you and victory in your name. I will no longer be intimidated by long odds or impossible situations, for nothing is impossible with you, Lord.

Today's reading: Psalm 18

MONDAY

"You are light for the world. A city cannot be hidden when it is located on a hill. No one lights a lamp and puts it under a basket. Instead, everyone who lights a lamp puts it on a lamp stand. Then its light shines on everyone in the house. In the same way let your light shine in front of people. Then they will see the good you do and praise your Father in heaven." (Matthew 5:14–16)

For a long time my light was burning so low I didn't need to put it under a basket to hide it. But that light, my little light, was the only light I had. So you cleaned my glass, repaired my wick, added fresh oil and lit my light again. Now Lord, this little light of mine? "I'm gonna let it shine!"

Today's reading: Mark 4

TUESDAY

"Let your kingdom come. Let your will be done on earth as it is done in heaven." (Matthew 6:10)

Your kingdom is within the hearts of your people. Help me to continually acknowledge you as the King and Lord of my life. Thank you for allowing me to help in your kingdom's growth. Accomplish your will in my life today.

Today's reading: Luke 17

WEDNESDAY

"People don't pick grapes from thorn bushes or figs from thistles, do they? In the same way every good tree produces good fruit, but a rotten tree produces bad fruit. A good tree cannot produce bad fruit, and a rotten tree cannot produce good fruit. Any tree that fails to produce good fruit is cut down and thrown into a fire. So you will know them by what they produce." (Matthew 7:16–20)

Father, when tragedy struck my life almost a year ago, I thought my fruit bearing days were over. Now I can see the hopeful sign of spring blossoms in my branches, carrying the promise of sweet fruit once again. Thank you for infusing me with your life and restoring my sense of purpose.

Today's reading: Psalm 51

THURSDAY

"Jesus said to him, 'Whoever starts to plow and looks back is not fit for the kingdom of God.'" (Luke 9:62)

For many years I've plowed in the field of life, Lord. Then suddenly, a year ago, I laid my plow down and stopped plowing altogether. I didn't look back, I just couldn't see in front of me anymore. Now my vision is returning; I'm back on the plow and I see something I don't understand—I'm further down the field than when I got off the plow, and my furrow is straight.

Today's reading: Psalm 103

FRIDAY

"But the spiritual nature produces love, joy, peace, patience, kindness, goodness, faithfulness, gentleness and self-control. There are no laws against things like that. If we live by our spiritual nature, then our lives need to conform to our spiritual nature." (Galatians 5:22,23,25)

I want to live by my spiritual nature, Lord, and I need to be vitally united with you on a daily basis for this to happen. Produce these qualities in me like fruit on a tree, that others may taste and see that you, Lord, are truly good.

Today's reading: Galatians 5

SATURDAY

"His miraculous signs are impressive. He uses his power to do amazing things. His kingdom is an eternal kingdom. His power lasts from one generation to the next." (Daniel 4:3)

The power of your love, Lord, has done an amazing thing in me. A year ago, I was focused on my pain and my needs; now, though still aware of both, I am also aware of the pain and needs of others. My heart breaks for those who are just beginning their journey of grief, but I am able to be your hand extended in love.

Today's reading: Psalm 145

SUNDAY

"Blessed are those who recognize they are spiritually helpless. The kingdom of heaven belongs to them." (Matthew 5:3)

Spiritually helpless I came into this world, spiritually hopeful I will depart. In my desperation, I abandoned my foolish pride and acknowledged that I was utterly helpless to fix my spiritual condition. On that day, you came to live inside of me and gave me the kingdom of heaven.

Today's reading: John 3

MONDAY

"Blessed are those who are gentle. They will inherit the earth." (Matthew 5:5)

Lord, you have taught me about gentleness by the gentle way you have walked with me for the last year. Now it is my turn to walk softly, care deeply and touch gently. With the same gentleness I experienced from you, I will go and be gentle to others who are going through the furnace of affliction. I won't be critical or judgmental. You have called me to love and be gentle and leave the judging to you. I will be your loving hand to a hurting world.

Today's reading: 2 Samuel 22

TUESDAY

"Blessed are those who hunger and thirst for God's approval. They will be satisfied." (Matthew 5:6)

I've never been more vulnerable than I've been this past year, Lord. And during that time, I needed desperately to have a sense of your unconditional approval. You gave that to me years ago, when I first came to know you, but I can't tell you how much it meant to me that you never withdrew your approval and acceptance of me even when some of my actions were foolish. Lead me, Lord, in your paths of approval.

Today's reading: Philippians 3

WEDNESDAY

"Blessed are those who show mercy. They will be treated mercifully." (Matthew 5:7)

If I've learned one thing this year, I've learned mercy! When I came to the end of myself, I encountered your limitless mercy. When I stumbled down this darkened pathway, I met mercy. When I thought you had abandoned me, I found mercy. When I failed miserably, your mercy was waiting. Your mercy, O Lord, endures forever! Now, I will be your message of mercy to a frightened and confused world.

Today's reading: Psalm 136

THURSDAY
"Blessed are those whose thoughts are pure. They will see God."
(Matthew 5:8)

It seems Lord, that suffering a loss like this has a way of bringing that which is impure to the surface of my life so that it may
be seen for what it is and removed, leaving only that which is
pure. In this last year, it seems I've been going through a puri-
fication process, one that is still far from complete. But as
the impurities are removed, I begin to see you, not in some
heavenly form, but in the eyes of the desperate and lonely.
And when I see those eyes, I remember having that look in my
own eyes, and weep. Send me, Lord.

Today's reading: Psalm 24

FRIDAY
*"Blessed are those who make peace. They will be called God's
children."* *(Matthew 5:9)*

I remember thinking peace would never come to my heart.
Turmoil and fear wrapped in grief seemed to chase my peace
away. But I found that as I lingered in your presence and lis-
tened to your words of hope, the tide of peace began to rise
again. It was slow and gentle, but unstoppable. Now it fills

my heart, and others are calmed by its quiet reassuring strength. I will be your conduit of peace to a troubled world.

Today's reading: John 6

SATURDAY
"Blessed are those who mourn. They will be comforted." (Matthew 5:4)

When I began my mourning a year ago, I did not think I could find comfort. I was much like a burn victim. Nothing could soothe the pain, and I couldn't foresee the pain ever subsiding. Now a year later, the scars from my burn are clearly visible and the new skin is tender to the touch, but I have found comfort and healing for my soul. There is more healing ahead and more comfort to be had, but with the comfort I have experienced, I will comfort others and give them the most precious gift you gave me … grace for grief.

> *"That is why whenever other people suffer,*
> *we are able to comfort them by using*
> *the same comfort we have received from God."*
> (2 Corinthians 1:4)